THE E-COMMERCE REVOLUTION

Changes that have been driven by COVID-19

How such a horrible thing can grow other's wealth?

Copyrights © 2021 by Dominika Smialkiewicz

All rights reserved. No part of this publication may be reproduced, distributed, or transmitted in any form or by any means, including photocopying, recording, or other electronic or mechanical methods, without the prior written permission of the publisher, except in the case of brief quotations embodied in critical reviews and certain other noncommercial uses permitted by copyright law. For permission requests, contact the author through the website below.

E-commerce Entrepreneur

http://ecommpreneur.eu

Table of Contents

Your Free Gift 1

Chapter 1 2
   Introduction To The Concept Of E-Commerce 2

Chapter 2 11
   History Of E-Commerce 11

Chapter 3 18
   Revolution And Evolution Of E-Commerce 18

Chapter 4 29
   Quarantines And Online Shopping 29

Chapter 5 47
   A Virtual Connection 47

Chapter 6 59
   Impact Of Covid-19 On E-Commerce Industry.......... 59

Chapter 7 82
   Covid-19 And Amazon Sellers 82

Chapter 8 99
    A Trigger For The Turning Point Of E-Commerce 99
Chapter 9 109
    Growing Importance Of E-Commerce In A Post-Covid World 109
Chapter 10 121
    Future Of E-Commerce 121
Conclusion.. 125

YOUR FREE GIFT

I HAVE SOMETHING FOR YOU. It won't cost you a dime. It's a 20-page e-book titled "Catapult Your E-Sales! The Top 10 Things You Must Develop To Get More Money Online." I'd like you to have a free copy with my thanks.

You can grab your copy by clicking on the following link and joining my mailing list:

http://ecommpreneur.eu/free-gift/

You got The E-Commerce Revolution with the expectation that I would explain to you how and why did the Covid-19 have a huge impact on the e-commerce area. I appreciate your confidence in me. This is my way of saying thank you.

Chapter 1

Introduction To The Concept Of E-Commerce

E-COMMERCE:

E-commerce is an abbreviation for electronic commerce. If internet is used to buy and sell and something, that is known as E-commerce. E-Commerce is very much in practice in the world today. People favor buying stuff online more as compared to going to the shops physically. E-commerce is more convenient and much practiced by people all around the world. It allows you to shop anything you want and wish for from any retailer, no matter which country or region they belong from.

Many brands and businesses have transitioned to the online retail business because it is easier for them to reach out to the intended customers and clients. Not just that, but the customers also prefer online shopping more in comparison to shopping and buying stuff physically.

DIFFERENT E-COMMERCE MODELS:

Different e-commerce models that are commonly being used by the type of participants that are involved in the process are given below:

1. Business to Business Model
2. Business to Consumer Model
3. Consumer to Consumer Model
4. Direct to Consumer Model
5. Consumer to Business Model

1. BUSINESS TO BUSINESS MODEL:

Business-to-business model is the type of e-commerce model in which two businesses carry out trade and sell their products to each other. These businesses may also sell their products to the wholesalers and retailers. A business sells goods or services to another business and this type does not involve dealing with any consumer. In business-to-business e-commerce, the businesses usually sell products like raw materials, software, etc. Manufacturers also sell to the retailers directly in the business-to-business e-commerce model.

2. BUSINESS TO CONSUMER MODEL:

Unlike the business-to-business model, in the business-to-consumer model, the businesses sell their products to potential consumers. They target their consumers and manufacture products that are of interest to them. Business-to-consumer model is very much in use as compared to the other business models. Here the businesses sell their products to the consumers. For example, you buy some furniture from an online retail shop.

3. CONSUMER TO CONSUMER MODEL:

Consumer to consumer model is the type of e-commerce model in which the consumers sell and buy from each other online. Market places like Fiverr, Etsy, etc., offer consumer-to-consumer businesses.

4. DIRECT TO CONSUMER MODEL:

In direct to consumer model, the businesses deal with the consumers directly. There are no wholesalers, retailers, or distributors involved in the process of selling goods or services to the consumers. The brands or businesses directly sell the goods to their customers. Such sales happen on social media websites like Snapchat, Instagram, Facebook, etc. Selling platforms provide subscriptions, and because of those subscriptions, the selling and buying are done. This eliminates all the third parties that have been previously involved in the process.

5. CONSUMER TO BUSINESS MODEL:

Consumer-to-business is another business model which is being used by the businesses and the consumers both. In consumer-to-business model, an individual offers its services to any business. This can be photographers, freelancers, etc.

EXAMPLES OF E-COMMERCE:

The common types of e-commerce are given below:

1. **RETAIL:**

   Retail is the type of e-commerce in which the products are directly sold to the customers. There is no third party involved in doing business.

2. **DROPSHIPPING:**

   Another type of e-commerce is that of dropshipping. In dropshipping when a company or business sells products, they do that via a third party. The products after they are manufactured are shipped over to the customers via an intermediator. The products are not directly sold to the customers or the consumers.

3. **DIGITAL PRODUCTS:**

   The commonly practiced business in the e-commerce is that of the digital products. Items that can be easily downloaded, like e-books, templates and other online courses, etc. can be purchased for a long time use. A large percentage of the e-commerce transactions constitute of the selling and buying of these digital products.

4. **SUBSCRIPTIONS:**

You subscribe to the products or the services that are used on a regular basis. These subscriptions to services are also one of the most commonly used methods of direct business with the customer.

5. **WHOLESALE:**

In wholesale, the products are sold in bulk, usually to a retailer. The retailer then sells the products to the customers.

6. **SERVICES:**

Services like online coaching and writing etc. are provided. They are purchased and paid for online.

7. **CROWDFUNDING:**

Crowdfunding is a method that allows the sellers to raise money for their startups. By raising money for their startup, they are able to bring their product to the market. After collecting, the customers purchase the product. Once enough customers have purchased the item it is then created and shipped to the consumers.

FAMOUS E-COMMERCE WEBSITES:

There are a lot of famous websites that allow you to purchase or sell any product. These websites are like marketplaces. These websites make it easier for consumers to purchase or sell anything they want. Famous websites that are commonly used by both consumers and businesses to sell and buy products are mentioned below. All this process of selling and buying happens online without visiting any markets physically. This convenient method of shopping and selling is gaining more popularity among the masses, brands, and businesses alike.

1. **ALIBABA:**

    Alibaba is a Chinese company that was launched back in 1999. It is one of the most famous and commonly used e-commerce and retailer. It is a marketplace that handles different types of business to business, consumer to consumer, and business to consumer services. Alibaba marketplaces are all over the globe and also are the most efficient ones. The sales of Alibaba have been the highest among all the US retailers, in fact, they have surpassed those of the US retailers and online marketplaces.

2. **AMAZON:**

    Amazon is a marketplace that offers different types of services for buying and selling goods. It is a marketplace that the people buy frequently from and is considered as a large retailer website in the United States. Many companies want to beat the amazon when it comes to sales.

3. **EBay:**

    EBay is among the pioneering websites of E-Commerce which people turned to when they wanted to sell or purchase products online. EBay is still considered to be one of the most dominant and successful websites for online business. Individuals and businesses use it to sell their products online.

4. WALMART:

Walmart offers subscriptions and also get your groceries delivered to you at your doorstep. It is as famous as the other online retailers. Walmart is considered to be one of the top retailer sites for online purchasing and selling.

5. WAY FAIR:

Way Fair is one of the top online retailers for purchasing and selling home furniture. Not just is it an online home furnishing retailer but also a drop-shipper. They personalize and develop those products which they personally believed are well liked by the customers.

BENEFITS OF E-COMMERCE:

E-commerce comes with numerous benefits. Some of the huge benefits that come with the online shopping and retail are:

1. CONVENIENCE:

Online shopping and selling products online are convenient. That is why one of the topmost benefits of e-commerce is convenience. The purchases become simple and consume less time. They can be done at any time and whenever you are free you can purchase online.

2. CUSTOMER SUPPORT:

The odds of brand loyalty and authenticity are greatly improved if the customers are allowed to personalize their products. These e-commerce websites allow them to interact with the brand owners and business owners on a very different and personal level. Customer support is highly enhanced in these e-commerce marketplaces. The people who shop from these marketplaces feel understood by the brands because they can personalize and customize whatever and however they want.

3. ACCESSED FROM ALL OVER THE WORLD:

You can be provided access to any brand, local or international of your own liking and choice. These e-commerce marketplaces allow you to buy from any brand from all over the world. The geographical barrier is no longer present. That makes the user experience even better.

4. REDUCED COSTS:

Since you can buy anything you want with just one click. You do not have to travel for whatever you want to buy. This saves a lot of your time and expenses. These online marketplaces help you with cost reduction and no wastage of time. You can purchase anything you wish and whenever you wish. This not just benefits the consumer but the businesses as well. They would not be required to set up stores and invest in those. Digital sellers can launch their websites with little to no cost. They would just require to have an inventory for manufacturing and storing of the products. Good and promising promotions can help them grow their business a lot even if they do not have any stores physically from which the customers can buy. Online stores can help them as well.

COVID-19 AND E-COMMERCE:

Covid-19 has shut down many businesses that were previously running smoothly because of the economic losses that different countries had to face because of the pandemic. But it has surely escalated the e-commerce sales on different online retailer websites. People have been more inclined towards shopping online. It has greatly increased sales of different products and companies. Recent statistics show how sales have been rising in the pandemic. While the economy may have been affected but this pandemic had been a piece of good news for many business owners who have established their online businesses and do all the purchasing and selling over these e-commerce websites. In this book, we shall closely see and observe how the pandemic resulted in the escalation of the businesses that happen online.

Chapter 2

History Of E-Commerce

E-commerce is a common practice now, and a lot of people have been a part of this online system of purchasing and selling. Also, due to the recent Covid-19 pandemic, e-commerce sales have been increased multiple folds. A lot of people have started to purchase stuff online rather than going to the shops physically. A number of businesses have gained profit because of these great sales happening. Before we move on to the impact of the covid-19 pandemic on these online businesses, we will discuss a little bit about the history of the origin of these online business websites. In the olden times, these online businesses were not so popular, and then slowly and gradually as time passed by and technology progressed, a rise in the popularity of online stores and businesses was observed. Brief information on how e-commerce was originated and when and why this all began is stated below.

If we looked back some decades ago, we would see that the concept of e-commerce never existed. E-commerce originated and developed with the inception of the internet. Ever since technology progressed and the internet got introduced, the concept of e-commerce was developed as well. Around 40 years ago, when the early data interchange (EDI) got introduced, it paved the way for what we now know as e-commerce. Due to its widespread and multiple benefits in no time, it became known to all. The concept existed but was still not in a practical state to continue with because, as we already discussed that the internet and e-commerce online websites are closely intertwined. Online shopping was available for the common public only when the internet was made available to the common public back in 1991. In the United States, Amazon was the first online retailing website that was launched for online shopping. Soon after, other businesses followed too. A lot of businesses have now become involved in online dealing with not just the customers but other businesses as well.

INCEPTION OF ONLINE SHOPPING:

Michael Aldrich was the inventor of online shopping. He invented it in the year 1979. Michael belonged to the United Kingdom. He was successful in using a telephone line to connect a television which was modified to a real-time multi-user transaction processing system. In 1980, the system was brought into marketing and sold to the United Kingdom, Ireland, and Spain. It was mainly a business to business system.

An online book store was developed by Charles M. Stack by the name of Book Stacks Unlimited in the year 1992. It was a dial-up bulletin that was founded three years before Amazon came into the business. After the internet availability and worldwide usage, the book store also transitioned to the internet as Books.com. Books.com was later acquired by Barnes and Noble.

FIRST ONLINE TRANSACTION:

The first online transaction happened in the year 1992. In a New York Times issue of August 12, 1994, an article was published which shared the first sale transaction guaranteeing complete privacy. Two cyberspace entrepreneurs developed an already existing software into a stronger and secure software for data transactions. The cyberspace entrepreneurs who managed to do this were celebrated.

TIMELINE OF E-COMMERCE:

This timeline would cover all that happened from the inception of e-commerce in its early days.

EARLY '60s UP TILL EARLY '80s:

The e-commerce concept first originated in the early '60s. After the coming out of the Electronic Data Interchange (EDI). The EDI helped in replacing the fax into digital transferring of the data from one computer to another. Later then Aldrich managed to shop from their local store by using the television to their departmental store to deliver groceries at their house. It sparked a new concept of teleshopping.

EARLY '80s UP TILL 1990:

Because of these advancements, it was clear that the business could be possible but the business to a customer could not be implemented because at that time the business to customer dealing was not possible and nor was it successful because of the lack of PCs and the internet. Internet was not yet available for the common public to use.

A few of the early platforms that were used for e-commerce purposes are stated as follows. France launched Minitel, Minitel would connect people from all over the world through telephone lines.

Those who subscribed to the telephone services could use the service freely. Also, the terminal which was used to access the telephone lines was videotex. It was a popular system that people used, but after a few years, the internet emerged, and people switched to internet facilities and Minitel lost its popularity along the way.

THE EARLY 90s:

Internet became known to people during the early 90s. In the year 1991, common public was allowed to use the internet. People transitioned to the internet and the World Wide Web became the talk of the town. People also started using it for commercial purposes and in no time became popular but there was a security issue that came along. To address that issue, a security protocol was developed. The Secure Socket Layer (SSL) was developed which made sure that whatever transactions that were made on the internet while shopping online remained confidential and secure. The Secure Socket Layer protocol was important to be installed for authenticity. The web browsers would be able to identify if the Secure Socket Layer protocol has been installed and whether this site can be trusted or not. The Secure Socket Layer is still very common in use. It is an important part of web security. A new version of the Secure Socket Layer protocol has been released which is used to ensure security and protection of the websites and also ensure the safety of transactions in e-commerce.

THE MID '90s UP TILL NOW:

Ever since the internet emerged, it has upped the e-commerce game. With the progression in technology and the internet, e-commerce has been becoming even more popular. A lot of people are showing more and more interest in online shopping because all the dealings can be done with just a click on your phone. If we look back at the mid and late '90s, an upward trend in the e-commerce sector was observed. Amazon was the first e-commerce site that was launched and it is even now considered as the most frequently used and successful websites of E-Commerce ever launched. Amazon got launched and became popular after the internet was available to the common public. Just because Amazon was not a physical store, it provided many offers to its customers, the variety and diversity among the product range available on Amazon could be seen. Ever since then, Amazon has been an online retailer company that people would trust with their eyes closed. Even now, customer reviews are a common practice on Amazon where people who bought from the website share their experiences. These customer reviews are beneficial for other people who want to order or buy from Amazon as well, it builds trust in the seller that they are selling authentic stuff. The product availability on Amazon has been multiplied multiple folds since it became popular among the masses. They now also offer music, video, downloads, apparel, etc.

Not just Amazon but Etsy and eBay are also websites that are commonly used by clients and customers to buy stuff from. eBay was launched in 1995, whereas Etsy was launched back in 2005. Other platforms were also launched for merchants in the late '90s. These platforms were able to distribute their products for sale in the late '90s. In 2005, Amazon launched Amazon Prime. Amazon Prime came with subscription services. An annual fee was required to pay in order to avail the membership for shipping the products in just two days all across the United States. This subscription offers also pressurized other merchants and sellers to work more on their shipping and delivery services to make them more efficient.

MOBILE E-COMMERCE:

Mobile E-commerce was first introduced back in 1997. The use of mobile phones has increased more than ever nowadays, so as a result, it gained popularity almost two decades. People nowadays prefer using their mobile phones for the daily transactions for their day-to-day chores that are needed to be done. Mobile devices also allow you to have a better customer experience and support. Mobile sales have reached up to 54 percent of the sales, this 54 percent is among all the e-commerce sales that will happen until the end of 2021. This shows how popular mobile sales have become and how much people prefer using these devices. Businesses are now well promoted due to the increased use of social media, this leaves a lot of room for personalization and customization as per the needs of the customer. All the businesses and customers alike have been turning to the use of mobile devices for the purpose of enhancing their e-commerce experience. These mobile devices have also made it easy to research products and coupons. As they are becoming popular day by day, the business buyers are also expecting that more features would be introduced so it can make the whole experience better.

Chapter 3

Revolution And Evolution Of E-Commerce

REVOLUTION OF E-COMMERCE:

E-commerce has been revolutionized ever since its inception. It is no longer the same as it was a few decades before. Everything is different than it was before. Everyone is in favor of online shopping and these websites provide you a platform to shop the products. The businesses which use these platforms to sell their products also contribute to making e-commerce more revolutionary and evolutionary. Constant efforts are made to make the experience of online shopping convenient and easy for both buyers and sellers. In the past, internet availability and accessibility were not as common as it is nowadays. The availability of the internet has made all these experiences way better than they were before. Due to the internet, it has become very easy and also it has been made possible to achieve whatever you want in your business. It opens up the door to countless opportunities and ways to enhance your business.

E-commerce has been revolutionized in some phases, let me discuss these phases to have a better understanding of its evolution.

BEGINNING OF REVOLUTION OF E-COMMERCE:

In the beginning, the businesses thought that no matter whatever products they bring into the market, they will be welcomed by the customers and buy them. So they would work hard and make as much product as they could. The sellers had a misconception that no matter what, the customers would always buy from them. This very negatively impacted the businesses because the customers did not buy all that would be made available to them. They had no idea about marketing strategies, what can they do to make their business sustainable because what they were doing was not something that would make their business sustainable. They knew nothing about their targeted audience, they used to initially pay zero attention to the customer support or user experience. They were of the view that it is the internet and no matter what they sell on the internet people would end up buying them. They just looked at one picture and completely ignored the other. They started uploading every product on the internet and made it available to people. They kept updating about the quantity and other descriptions of the products. Managing the products and making them available, not just that but at the same time making sure that all the buyers or customers are entertained, was also an overwhelming job to do. There were issues with the whole process but just because it was a new experience for the users and the businesses alike, people started enjoying this new experience of online shopping.

PHASE 1 OF BRINGING REVOLUTION IN E-COMMERCE:

During this phase, the business owners started to think about their businesses. They realized that what they are doing right now is not benefitting them. They also realized that they are going to exhaust their resources if they keep on developing the products without any business marketing strategies. Businesses need to take special care of customer experience because of its great importance. The customers are going to come back to your store if you provide them with good customer support policies. If once the customers get disappointed in some brand, they tend to never return and shop from them again. The business, after realizing the fact that they need to improve their user experience and customer support joined hands with different companies for enhancing their user experience aspect. There are multiple companies available that provide you with better and improved templates that can help you with your own internet store. If you will be able to provide the users with a prominent user experience, it would be easier for them to go through all the products that are available in your store. It would be able to make them see the efforts you are putting in to make their shopping experience smooth and improved. Companies like woo-commerce stores and Shopify stores are going to help you with the templates for your own web store. These companies provide you with templates that are very efficient and improved. The users would get recommendations from the web stores as per their choice, and they would be able to personalize and customize their orders as per their liking. Your web store would become highly responsive and optimizable thus making the shop experience the users better and smooth. It would make them trust your brand and would not resist coming back to your store for more shopping. Previously not much attention was paid to these things because people were just excited about this new experience which these platforms were offering them regarding online shopping. This was a whole new concept back then but nowadays, it has become very common and there is no room for any errors. Growth is important for sustainability. You have to make sure that your business is sustainable. So in order to make it sustainable you always have to strive for perfection and improvement. So you have to grow according to the wishes and needs of your customers because it is them who are spending money and buying your products which in turn brings you profit. If the customers are spending on your products, you need to make sure that you are providing them with better and enhanced ways to help them have a smooth shopping experience. So many stores have now come into this field of online selling so if you do not improvise your store from time to time it is really going to affect your business. You have to keep thinking and implementing unique and innovative ideas in order to survive in this field, else you will be brought down by your competitors in no time. This is something about which the businesses should think from the beginning. This has been a very important step towards the evolution of the e-commerce industry.

PHASE 2 OF BRINGING REVOLUTION IN E-COMMERCE:

The usage of cell phone devices has increased multiple folds as compared to the past and it has been increasing ever since. Every person now has a cell phone in their hands. These cell phones are also used to purchase and sell products. The number of people using cell phones is alarmingly increasing and this is a wake-up call for the business to step up in whatever they are doing. Statistics show that the number of people who use their mobile phones for purchasing from online shops is around 1.8 billion. These 1.8 billion people are from all over the world because the trend for online shopping is now observed in each and every country. It is no longer confined to the developed or first world countries. Statistics also show that 63 percent of shopping occasions begin online. They prefer to look up the trends in fashion and other items online for convenience. Not just that but 62 percent of the people shop online at least once per month. The ongoing covid-19 pandemic has also affected the physical shopping experiences of people, so they prefer to shop online. This online shopping trend which has been observed during this pandemic, also shows how much people now prefer online shopping. These statistics regarding online shopping show that now the businesses have to make sure that they are bringing innovation in what they are doing. E-commerce is a field with strong competitors. If you do not work on your growth and do not succeed in bringing innovation in what you are doing you would not be able to achieve what you are wishing. In order to become successful in your business, you don't have to stick to the old methods. Covid-19 has also increased the demand for online shopping. The escalation in sales that have been observed in the e-commerce sector is a lot. This can make us think that online shopping surely has a bright future and is going nowhere but here to stay. So in order to stay relevant, you need to use the latest trends to make your business flourish.

PHASE 3 OF BRINGING REVOLUTION IN E-COMMERCE:

Now that the business owners have realized the importance of these ways of improving their businesses, they have started to invest huge amounts of money in bringing their businesses to that level where they can lead a road to success. They have started collaborating with different companies to provide them with improvised templates to work on because that is the need of time. Customer care is really important and there should be no compromise on that. Business strategies are also very important. You need to have strong strategies that you can use to attract more customers. The more customers you attract, the more your will brand become successful. Customers would give positive reviews that would help to bring more people to trust your brand. Trust of the customers is of great importance because if the customers would not trust you they would not come back to purchase from you. You need to present a good picture so you are able to attract as many people as you can to buy from your brand. Targeting your customers is also something you should not forget if you are a business owner. You need to see that the products you are selling, people belonging to which age groups are most interested in it. If you are a clothing brand for women, you would see women being your targeted customers. There will be women belonging from different age groups, funky and modern cuts are usually preferred by young age girls, and light colors and simple cuts are preferred by women belonging to women of middle age. So you have to identify your targeted customers and then see what design is or fabric that is more in demand. If any product is in high demand, you would have to pay more attention to producing that so you don't run out of stock. But that does not mean that you do not pay attention to the other products you have. You need to produce that product in good quality as well. Quality of the product matters, if you are not selling good quality products, do not expect people who buy from you once to come back to you again. You have to move forward and progress your business as the technology does. You have to keep up your pace with the progression and innovation in technology, if you slow down a bit, you would lag behind and your business would land in hot waters. The pace with which innovation is happening very soon, you would see robots taking over the jobs of humans. Even now amazon has started utilizing robots for packaging. The packaging department is conjointly controlled by robots. This would save manpower and time. This workforce could be utilized in something that the robots are unable to do.

SOCIAL MEDIA- A KEY FACTOR:

Social media has been a key factor in bringing about the much needed revolution of the e-commerce industry. Many businesses have accounts on different social media platforms that allows them to promote their products and also help them with interaction with their customers and clients. Social media platforms can be used to market and promote your product in a way in which you could not have promoted or marketed without social media. It is also very helpful with staying in contact with your clients. Your clients can tell you about their needs and what do they want for you in detail. They can customize the order as per their needs and wishes. The revolution which social media has brought about in the e-commerce industry is really important.

ONLINE ACCOUNTS FOR PAYMENTS AND TRANSACTIONS:

Online accounts that are used for payments for buying something online from these online marketplaces or transactions from retrieving money that you earn by selling products over these marketplaces are also a great initiative for revolutionizing the e-commerce industry. These online accounts are now on a rise because of the continuously growing online shopping trends. It is easy to pay for the products that are bought from these marketplaces online. This has made the lives of people convenient. The businesses also get the money in time so they can start the production and then the shipping process of the order to the intended customers. Due to these online payment accounts, you can transfer funds with ease and limitations that come with sending the funds online. The limitations are completely avoided if you are transferring funds. Also transferring and receiving funds through these online accounts take no time. You are able to transfer funds from one part of the world in a matter of minutes. These online payment accounts are simple to use and can be accessed from anywhere through your mobile phone.

ELECTRONIC CARDS:

Electronic cards are a great initiative in bringing ease to the whole process of online payments. They have greatly helped in evolving the e-commerce industry. If you have an electronic card issue from your bank, you can use that card to pay for any service online. You can do that with great ease and convenience. You do not have to visit your bank for each transaction. You can make these transactions from your bank account by using your cards. Online payments and transactions have also evolved greatly as compared to the traditional methods that were used in the past. These plastic cards are durable and make your life easy up to a great extent.

THE EVOLUTION OF E-COMMERCE HAS MADE EVERYTHING ACCESSIBLE:

The evolution of e-commerce has dissolved borders. You can now shop from any brand that you want to. Be it any local brand or international brand. You can get your hands on any international brand you want to as well. You can buy whatever you want to from any international retail brand through these marketplaces. You are given multiple options to shop from any brand or business that you are interested in or like. All that can happen even if you are sitting You just have to open the online web stores of those brands and get your shopping done. The payment can also be done very easily. You don't have to go through the hassle of payments as it can also be done online with your online payment accounts or your electronic cards issued from your banks. Business is no longer restricted because of the geographical borders because they longer exist if you are shopping online. This also helps the businesses a lot. They get the opportunity to marketing and promoting their brand globally. This is one of the great evolution that has been brought to the e-commerce industry.

If the brands and businesses are dealing with customers from across the globe and not just one geographical territory, they have to put extra efforts into making the whole shopping experience for their customers smooth. They should take extra care and try to eliminate all the potential barriers that could come in between them and the customers. If they manage to make the dealings with foreign clients and customers, they will become popular across the globe.

ESCALATED GROWTH AND REGULATIONS:

If a business is selling to customers from across the globe that would enhance their business and let it grow but there would be another issue of data safety and security. They will have to work more on that aspect so they are able to seal their dealings in a proper way. Regulatory steps are needed to be taken to ensure the data that the customers are providing. If the brands neglect these regulations to keep the data of the customers safe, it is highly likely they would find themselves under great problems. The brands and retailers who do not pay attention to these regulations will be exposed to penalties and risks. Privacy of the customers is something which the businesses need to protect at any cost. If they are looking to expand their businesses beyond the geographical borders onto different countries across the globe. This comes with great risks and these risks are very important to be mitigated because that is going to do irreplaceable damage to them. Privacy is very important and people do not usually compromise on the cybersecurity aspect.

Chapter 4

Quarantines And Online Shopping

Right when the year 2019 was about to end, the world witnessed something novel. A virus started affecting the lives of people drastically and within no time, the virus spread across the borders and slowly and gradually took the whole world in its control. After cases being reported from all over the world, World Health Organization declared it as an emergency and a pandemic. This pandemic caused by the covid-19 drastically changed the lives of everybody on the face of the earth. Heartbreaking and scenes that would break a person's heart were seen in the entire world. No country was safe from this novel coronavirus. The virus spread like wildfire, sending countless people to hospitals because of their critical condition and as many to their graves. The death toll of the coronavirus is very high. A lot of people have been tested positive for the virus. The situation in most of the countries that did not have a strong health care system has deteriorated. Not just the countries with weak health care facilities have suffered but countries like the United States and other developed countries where the health care system is exemplary have also greatly suffered at the hands of this pandemic. Nobody is safe, be it young adults or aged people, be it the rich or poor, everyone has suffered alike. As it is a contagious virus and can spread if an infected person comes in close proximity to a healthy person. So in order to reduce and stop the spread of this virus, many countries announced complete lockdowns. They announced complete lockdowns bringing all the business activities to a halt. The lives of people across the world have also been at a halt because they can no longer leave their houses. They are directed to stay inside their houses to reduce contact with other people as much as possible. Work from home has been a common practice that was observed when the cases of coronavirus reached their peak. People were advised and directed to stay inside their house and to limit their contact with the outer world. They were also instructed by their governments to avoid traveling and stay inside their houses.

This lockdown and self-quarantine which they had to go through greatly affected their mental health. They had to go through many psychological problems as well. They adopted some practices which they would not have otherwise. One of them is online shopping. As the rise in coronavirus cases was reported from all across the world so did the rise in sales at these online marketplaces was reported. People indulged in online shopping sprees. The percentage of sales that have been increased during this quarantine and lockdown situation has escalated pretty quickly. Despite the fact that lockdowns imposed throughout the world greatly affected other businesses which are not available online and a loss in the economic situation was observed. Businesses that are not done through these online marketplaces but in the physical markets were affected a lot and those merchants always protested against the lockdowns because of their businesses but were unfortunately closed down due to the ongoing corona situation. Also, due to the increasing cases of the covid-19 pandemic, people felt more scared and terrified while going to physical shops.

Now let me discuss why was there a rise in the sales over these online marketplace during the lockdown and quarantine situation:

1. **BOREDOM:**

   A big reason why people could not stop themselves from buying online marketplaces is boredom. Because of the limited to no contact with the outer world, people would spend most of their time inside their houses. Most of the work schedules got changed and the practice of work from home was adopted. Because of that, they would just go to different shopping sites and would end up buying from those websites impulsively. This was a psychological effect which this lockdown and quarantine situation had on their minds. An empty mind is a devil's workshop. Quarantine and lockdown situation has greatly decreased the pace of everyday life. People now have more free time im comparison to the past, before the Covid-19 pandemic hit the world. Because of this reason, people have started to feel boredom striking and this boredom led them to impulsive buying. They end up spending their savings.

2. ONLINE SHOPPING FELT SAFER:

People preferred online shopping from these internet marketplaces because they felt it was safe. Rather than going to the physical shops, ordering and purchasing from these online retail shops felt safer. Also due to the closing down of the physical shops people had no other option left but to purchase from these online retailers. If they had to go to some shop physically they would have come in contact with several other people which would have exposed them to the coronavirus and increased their chances of being affected by it. So a safe practice to follow, this way you would also be able to follow all the protocols that are necessary in order to avoid the virus getting in contact with you. You would be able to maintain your distance from other people. Many businesses have transitioned to the online system in order to keep their customers and employees safe from the coronavirus. They now offer online services so that the customers are able to order online whatever they want to buy and get it delivered to their doorstep without letting them leave their houses. This way they are able to abide by the health and safety precautions.

3. ONLINE SHOPPING HELPED SMALL BUSINESSES:

Just as we have seen multiple businesses being affected by the lockdown situation in different parts of the world, there we have also seen small businesses and startups flourishing. Just because of the free time that people are having in this lockdown situation they have decided to make use of their skills and put them to use. A lot of small businesses have emerged during the quarantine period. Online shopping has also allowed them to make their businesses successful because people buy from them. This way they are able to make their businesses thrive and are taking full advantage of this situation. These small business owners have been lucky in terms of online shopping, they are exhibiting and putting their skills to use and are helping their businesses grow. In these uncertain times due to the support of their new and old customers, they are able to generate their normal incomes and are able to provide for their families. People preferring to shop online also end up helping these businesses that have been in uncertain and bad conditions because of the ongoing pandemic.

4. **YOUR ORDER IS DELIVERED AT YOUR DOORSTEP:**

Another reason why online shopping has been greatly preferred by people and its sales getting increased as a result is that they can have their order delivered at their doorstep. They are able to shop for all the essentials and other items by staying inside their houses and not leaving yet get everything that they want at their homes. This is a great way to keep themselves safe from uncertain outdoor situations. This allows them to keep themselves safe and also succeed in keeping their loved ones safe. People become less prone to exposure to the coronavirus. If they have an elderly person at their home, it is very important to make sure that all the precautions are strictly followed because they are highly likely to catch the disease and end up facing severe symptoms. This way they do not only do themselves a favor but also to those who they love and care for. If the parcel gets delivered, it can be made sure that it is properly disinfected and sanitized. After receiving the parcel, it is also advised to wash hands and make sure to keep the parcel in the sunlight for extra protection.

5. **IT IS CONVINIENT:**

Even before the spread of the covid-19, online shopping was still thought to be one of the most convenient ways of shopping. You do not have to leave your house and go to the stores to buy stuff when you can easily do that by staying inside your home and get everything that you need to be delivered to your doorstep. Those days are now talk of the past where one would go to the stores and walk through every aisle to get what they wanted. Now you can get everything that you want without leaving your bed. This is how convenient online shopping is. Now when the world is hit by a pandemic, the departmental and online retail stores have been shut down in order to slow the spread of Covid-19. Online shopping is more convenient because of the fact that people do not risk their safety and are able to follow all the precautionary measures and protocols.

6. **SAVES TIME:**

Online shopping saves a great deal of your time. The time that you would spend while traveling to and from the shop can be easily saved if one opts for online shopping. Also searching for each item in different sections can waste a lot of your time. The lockdown situation has restricted everyone to their houses which gives them more time to spend with family and their loved ones. Rather than going to the store to buy stuff when it can be easily purchased by using their mobile phone and then getting it delivered to their doorstep, they can indulge themselves in spending some quality time with their parents or have a little story time with their siblings. It can greatly help people come close to each other and help them enjoy as much time as possible with the people they are not usually able to.

7. **INCREASED USE OF SOCIAL MEDIA:**

Just because of the free time that people have on their hands because of these uncertain times, they tend to use social media a lot. Increased usage of social media influences them and if they see something pretty or nice they end up buying it without caring the fact if they need it or not. They usually end up buying stuff which is not a necessity but a wastage of money. Social media usage is also a cause of impulse online purchasing.

8. **STRONG MARKETING CAMPAIGNS BY BRANDS:**

Just now, we discussed how people have been using social media up to an extent where they end up impulsive buying stuff they do not even need. It may be your brain forcing you to buy stuff that you do not even need, but it is also the strong marketing campaigns that the brands and businesses are running. These brands have been spending a lot of money on coming up with these strategies and marketing campaigns where these ads keep popping up every now and then, you end up buying stuff from these online retailer sites. These brands are using the influencers by paying them so they drive their followers to their online stores. The marketing campaigns by these brands in collaboration with the influencers having a large following on their social media accounts is also one of the huge reasons for the increased sales of the online stores. These are different marketing strategies that these online retailers use in order to expand their businesses and attract more number od customers towards their brand. They have also made their stores more user-friendly so the users can easily access them through their mobile phones as well as their personal computers. They keep offering deals and bundles in order to keep the customers hooked. They also keep on posting eye-catching images of their products so that people are attracted to them. Also, different brands and businesses have come up with sales that drive the users into buying from them. These are all marketing strategies that these businesses are mindful of and thought about. All this may seem like a coping mechanism to you during these tough and testing times, but you are also becoming a victim of the marketing strategies of these companies whose sole purpose is to direct people to their websites and online stores.

9. **LOW PRICES:**

Online shopping may seem convenient, but it is not always reliable. It is never known what type of a brand is on the other side who you are going to deal. Sometimes there are incidents where people end up ordering from sites that may seem authentic and trustworthy but end up getting scammed. They sell products at very cheap prices and they trick people into thinking that they are getting a good quality product in less price. The product and the brand try their best in order to convince the buyer to buy from them. In some cases, when the prices have been reduced the buyer does not even need convincing because they are trying to get their hands on the cheaper items. Low and reduced prices do not always guarantee that the product that is going to be delivered is going to be worth it. Most of the time when the product gets delivered it is low in quality or not the same as that was shown in the images. These types of strategies are used and applied by the low-quality and those scamming brands whose sole purpose is to deceive the customers by selling them products of low quality.

HOW CAN THE BUSINESSES IMPROVE?

The common public because of the lockdowns and quarantines, has been spending time indoors. They are often observed to be indulging in online shopping for various reasons. They are either shopping impulsively or shopping out of necessity. But this is the trend that has been observed during the time when governments all over the world have been imposing lockdowns and asking people to stay inside their houses to limit their contact with other people. You never know who has been affected by the virus because sometimes people are infected, but they do not tend to show any symptoms. These lockdowns have been imposed to slow down or completely stop the spread of this novel virus. In order to make the experience of the people who are indulging in online shopping easy and comfortable the businesses have to make more efforts into providing ease and comfort to their customers. The times are already tough enough so if there is anything they can do to make these shopping experiences smooth and better they should not step back from doing that. If they would understand the sentiments and expectations that the customers have from any product, then the businesses should keep making changes accordingly in order to make their shopping experience better and smooth. This would also result in customers trusting the businesses. This way the businesses would be able to retain their customers as they would keep coming back and this would help the businesses make extra profit. Some of the ways through which the customers can be given a smooth experience of shopping online are stated below:

1. **DO NOT STOP MAKING EFFORTS IN CUSTOMER CARE:**

   You should always try to make customer care your priority. If your customers feel like they are given importance and special attention is paid to their needs and wants they will always keep coming back to you. Most businesses and brands lose their clients because they are unable to provide them with proper customer care. Customers are the main entity that brings about profits to the businesses so they should be treated well and cared for as well. You can keep track of their reviews about your brand on social media. The customers after getting products from your business or avail of your services, often post reviews about their experiences. Pay special attention to these reviews and look for any inconvenience that was caused to them. This would help you identify your negative points and you will be able to work on that in the future so you do not lose your clients and customers and they keep coming back to you. If a customer or client does not have a good experience with your business, they would speak about it to others and the word would go around, this would be a great setback for your business and your reputation will be ruined. So make sure the customers or clients who did not have a pleasant experience are compensated by providing them your best so they do not end up damaging or tarnishing the reputation of your brand. Always keep thinking of new ways on how you can provide your customers with great services. Thus customers would develop an emotional and loyal connection to your brand and will always put their trust in it, so make sure you do not stop your grind and making your customers feel heard and appreciated.

2. **MAKE SURE THE PRODUCTS ARE ALWAYS AVAILABLE:**

The times are tough and uncertain, but you need to be certain that you are making sure that the needs and demands of your customers are met. If any customer comes to your brand or business page to shop something and if that is not available or out of stock on your page, that would be a missed opportunity for your brand. That opportunity which you missed is highly likely to be going to your competitors. This will not only help your competing brand take advantage of what was missing on your website or page but also end up damaging your reputation. In order to avoid such situations, you need to have a close eye on your inventory and make sure that all the products and items are available for the customers to purchase. Customer satisfaction would get increased if you have everything that they need in stock. Keeping track of what is in your inventory is going to help you satisfy the products. The shipping and delivery of the products may take some time because of the pandemic, but you need to make everything at your end for the customers to be always ready. You can also use your statistics of the products that the customers usually buy and are high in demand. Your purchase histories also play an important role in identifying the items that are in demand, and once you identify them, you can order them in advance so they are readily available in your inventory. You also can increase the sales and make the shopping experience for the customers better by introducing sales and discounts. These discounts would attract more customers and that will only be benefitting you. You would be achieving profits and also be able to attract people other than your regular customers. You can help your customers by introducing such features that make their shopping experience smooth. Features like live chats, image search, and a better and improved user interface can greatly help the customers and your business alike. Attention is needed to be paid to these little things which businesses often neglect but it is these little and small things that bring about a huge difference to your profits and losses. You need to understand the fact that you have to keep growing and progressing so your business does not become obsolete, evolving your business trends as the technology evolves in order to ensure growth. This growth would help you in becoming one of the most trusted brands in the business, and this is important for the sustainability of your brand.

3. SPECIAL TREATMENT FOR THE REGULAR CUSTOMERS:

You need to have special packages for the people who regularly shop from your brand. If the customers realize that are given special treatment, then nothing would stop them from coming back to you. You need to devise a plan on how to treat your regular customers in a special way. If you do not have any plan for the special treatment of your customers, you need to have one as soon as possible. You can give them special incentives, and that would make them have more trust in you and they would feel special. Having a plan for your regular customers is going to attract other people as well. It is something that needs to be implemented if you want your business to grow and retain your customers.

You should devise a loyalty program that will be customized for your regular customers and they can benefit from it. That way they will not lose trust in your brand and will keep coming back because they know that they are valued. The plan that is to be devised shall be according to the needs of the customers. You need to identify your weak points and help strengthen your business or brand.

4. MAINTAIN GOOD COMMUNICATION WITH THE CUSTOMERS:

In order to help your customers during these uncertain times, you need to make sure that you are communicating with them proactively. There is so much uncertainty in the outside world where nobody knows what awaits next. You can communicate about your working hours, what time are you going to operate and what possible steps could be taken in order to keep the environment inside your store safe and clean. You can let your customers in on any of the sales that you have planned in the nearest future. You also need to announce every detail to your customers through social media platforms. This way the customers would be well informed. Another important thing which you as a business owner should remember is to stay prepared. You need to stay prepared for any possible situation that could be faced in the near future. You need to keep a close check over your stock in the inventory. Using logistics and the purchasing history of your website, make sure you have all the stock available at your store, so there is no shortage of the products in demand. You should know that people are staying indoors and have nothing much to do so they are more likely to shop. If a certain number of buyers have visited your online shop in the past months, you should be prepared for more buyers to visit your store this month and the upcoming months. The lockdowns are not being lifted any time soon. Social media platforms can really help you in maintaining communication with your customers. That is the easiest way. You can also try to communicate to them through email or live chat options available on the website.

5. **PROMOTIONAL POLICIES:**

You need to work endlessly on your promotional policies, especially during the pandemic. Because this is a time of crisis where nothing is certain. You can work on your policies and try to make them strong. Think of any marketing plans that can help you survive through this uncertain time period. You can come up with gift cards as one of your promotional policies. You can introduce e-gift cards that would allow you to retain your customers. These e-gift cards would guarantee you that the customers are going to place orders with you again and will shop from you in the near future. This is a very good tactic that you can use for the retention of your customers. This would also help you attract more customers and help you in achieving profit and keep your business running in these hard times.

6. **PROVIDING VIDEO STREAMING OF YOUR PRODUCTS:**

Another way that you could adopt to improve your sales and the whole shopping experience of your customer in the lockdown and quarantine situation where they are unable to visit the physical stores is to provide video streaming. Providing video streaming of your products would help your customers in seeing the quality and design of the product in a better way. You would be able to showcase your products in an efficient way which could be useful in enhancing your sales. If you see a customer interested in some product that is available on your website, you can arrange video streaming of that product so they are able to see it in a better way. Suppose you are running a beauty salon; you can help people by streaming some of your services to help people while maintaining the safety protocols. You can keep guiding them on how they can do the basic services themselves at their homes. You can charge a minimal amount for these services as well. This would help your cash flow as well, and also be of great help to the people who are stuck inside their houses in the quarantine situation. It is a win-win situation for both the businesses and the customers or clients. You can try to showcase those services that are very basic and also much in demand from your customers. You can help them and guide them on how they can do root touchups by not leaving their houses or basic services like shaping of eyebrows.

7. DISCOUNTS AND SALES:

You can come up with discounts and sales on different items. Not much, but even the little sales could help. This is going to attract more customers towards your business, and they can buy from you. Also, the people who are indulging in online shopping can also avail these discounts and the products that they shop from your business or brands would not be too heavy on their pockets. Discounts and sales can also be of favor to both the parties, the clients as well as the businesses.

Covid-19 pandemic has drastically changed the e-commerce trends. It has made a big change in the way people shop now. It would take time for the businesses and the customers alike to get used to this situation because this is the new normal now. The customers and the users both have to adapt to these changes as the governments have ordered people to maintain the social safety protocols. It is a hard time that businesses are facing. Due to the closing down of shops in the lockdowns they have now transitioned to online stores. They have to make extra efforts in order to retain their customers. Because of the protocols for maintaining social distance and in order to keep themselves and their loved ones safe, people rely more on online shopping. They can easily do it by staying inside their homes, thus avoiding any social contact. Online shopping is both convenient and takes up less of your time. The time which you would usually spend on shopping at physical stores can be utilized in something else. Businesses have to step their social media game up. They have to make extra efforts in maintaining a connection with their clients and come up with the marketing policies that are going to help survive their business. Everybody now has to learn how to live life in this new normal way. Measures as per keeping the social safety protocols in mind have to be taken so everybody remains protected and safe from the horrors of coronavirus. It is the duty of everyone to take responsible steps in maintaining safety standards and protocols. All these changes and the evolution that this situation has brought in the e-commerce industry is going to bring about a revolution, this global crisis is to be considered the beginning of the revolution that was a long time coming.

Chapter 5

A Virtual Connection

The world has come to a halt after the outbreak of the novel coronavirus. All the businesses have been greatly affected. Due to this reason, a lot of businesses have transitioned their business to online e-commerce websites. The common public has also started to prefer buying from these online stores rather than going to the physical shops. Most of the countries in the world are under strict lockdowns where they are not allowed to leave their houses unnecessarily. Because of these reasons, a virtual connection has been established between the customers and the businesses. Businesses need to make efforts in order to strengthen this virtual connection and make sure that they are providing a smooth experience to their customers. The customers may be under self-quarantine, but this does not mean that they should not be provided with excellent services from the brands that they shop. Because of the spread of the coronavirus all across the world, people have started to panic. In a panic state, they have started to shop excessively. They shopped for the future. A lot of stores online and the physical ones were seen struggling in providing the basic necessities like toilet papers, soaps, etc. Shortage of food items was also recorded on some websites and physical stores. The businesses were not ready for this panicking situation at that time, because all this was new to them and that was something which they had not seen before. But now they know what the situation is and how the uncertainty is increasing with every passing day. They need to prepare themselves for any such situation that may happen in the future. They need to make sure that their inventories are stocked up, and they have everything available in advance. If the customers know that the businesses and brands are already making efforts in order to make their shopping experiences smooth, they would put even more trust in them. This is a great way for businesses to retain their customers and also attract more people. Steps like these are crucial for businesses and brands if they want to be successful in the long run. They have to look at the needs and wants of their clients and provide them with all of them. This is a marketing strategy that would make them a sustainable business.

If you compare digital businesses and physical businesses, you would conclude that digital businesses are on the safer side. That is because they have the means to stay more connected to their customers, whereas in physical businesses it is not possible. That is because the physical shops and stores have been closed down due to lockdown enforced in order to slow down the spreading of covid-19. A lot of businesses have suffered financially, either in supply chain disruptions, lesser sales than usual, and also because their employees have been affected by the virus. They are not able to maintain the connection with the customers that is important for the retention of customers. But on the other hand, digital businesses have been flourishing and blooming like a lily. They have come up with new marketing strategies that are helping them deal with the uncertain situation that popped because of the spreading of coronavirus. Statistics show that the sales of digital sales have shot up to a great extent. Due to this, they are able to survive their businesses due to the pandemic.

Important techniques and tips that the owners of these online businesses have implemented in order to strengthen the virtual connection between the customers and them are stated below:

1. **WORKING TO CURB THE SPREAD OF VIRUS:**

   These businesses have started to run campaigns that could help slow down spreading of the coronavirus. They have been running digital campaigns and creating awareness among the masses and urging them to stay safe and also help others stay safe. They have been urging people to follow the SOP's and safety precautions that could help them stop the spread of coronavirus. They have been letting their customers know about their efforts to overcome the coronavirus that has been wreaking havoc all across the globe. They keep on reassuring their customers that they are following all the SOP and keep on sanitizing all the products that they sell. This is a great way to let their customers maintain their trust on them in these tough and trying times.

2. **SOCIAL MEDIA PRESENCE:**

Social media can play a very important role in business promotion. Brands and businesses have started to market their products on social media. This has helped them greatly because nowadays, everyone is using social media more than ever and that is a great way for these brands and businesses to market their products. They have started to collaborate with different social media influencers. These social media influencers have a great fan following and their followers trust what they say and recommend. They deliver and share their products in a very subtle way and also ways that are relevant to the situation nowadays due to the pandemic and lockdowns. This way brands work on maintaining the virtual connection with their customers because they receive promotional messages of the brands and businesses through these social media bloggers and influencers.

3. **PROVIDING VIRTUAL TOURS:**

Just because people cannot visit any physical stores, they have started to prefer online shopping more. It is an easy and convenient way to buy whatever they need and get that delivered to their doorstep. To maintain that virtual connection with their customers and strengthen it as well, they have started to provide virtual tours to their customers. This is a way in which they promote their businesses. The world is going 3D now and these businesses and brands have also resorted to these 3D technologies to help flourish their business and increase their sales during the lockdown period. This has given the customers the ability to visit any time they wish to. They have started to enjoy the new experiences that these brands are providing them. They also have started interactive sessions with their customers where the customers can interact with them which gives the customers the same experience that they get during the physical visits to these stores. 3D images of the products are also now launched on their websites that provides a view of the product from every angle. This helps them see the product clearly. This is how businesses are evolving with the evolution in technology. These virtual tours are very beneficial for restaurant owners and salon owners. These virtual tours provide the customers with a better and enhanced view of the hotel rooms or the services they are offering. Restaurant business owners can also benefit from this 3D virtual viewing technology. These virtual tours are a great way for them to make their businesses during this pandemic sustainable. E-commerce, due to these latest trends, has become more and more popular. The sales have been drastically increased due to these new features these businesses have been introducing to help improve and enhance their customer support and also giving them smooth and better experiences.

4. **SPECIAL ATTENTION TO THE ENTRY POINTS:**

As it is evident that online businesses cannot be accessed from a single point, but they may be accessed with multiple entry points. It can either be redirection from some other websites, social media marketing, advertisement campaigns, etc. These online businesses have started to pay special attention to these entry points.

By doing so the brands are able to keep a check from where more of the traffic is directed to their sites. They keep a close eye on these things. This is how they are able to identify their weak points and how they can work to turn them into something positive for their business. If more of the traffic to their page is directed from social media marketing, they start to focus more on these marketing campaigns. They invest even more money so that their posts are able to reach as many people as possible. This is how they increase the reach of their businesses. Also, if they notice that less traffic to their site is directed from any advertisement campaigns, they start to pay attention to that as well. They try to come up with new strategies on how they can improve their advertisements so the traffic on their website increases. And that is how they turn their weak points into something positive and how they are able to gain the advantage of their weak areas. These are very important ways which the brands have worked on, and they have somewhat become successful because due to covid-19, no other business industry has flourished as compared to e-commerce. They say necessity is the mother of invention and right now, e-commerce businesses and brands have become a necessity of people due to the uncertain conditions as a result of covid-19. The same is the case with these brands and businesses and they need to make money and profit in order to survive these harsh conditions. Thus they keep on working and implementing new strategies and ideas, so they are able to sustain in the industry.

5. INNOVATIVE IDEAS TO ENHANCE ENGAGEMENT:

A lot of businesses have come up with innovative ideas in which they can help engage the customers. Brands need to facilitate in the matter and come out of their comfort zones in order to strengthen that connection with the customers.

Netflix is an e-commerce platform that works on subscriptions. Customers avail subscriptions, and then they are able to access the services. It is a media platform that provides you with media entertainment. Recently Netflix has come up with an innovative idea. They have introduced a new feature in order to give their customers the experience which they could not have due to the social safety protocols. Netflix has come up with a feature called Netflix Party. Using this feature, you can watch shows and movies with your friends at the same time and also chat and interact with each other. Friends can joke around, comment, or laugh at jokes together. This gives users the same experience that they would have if they were all present in one room and having fun. These get-togethers are no longer possible, thanks to covid-19. So this is an innovative and a great way to have a somewhat similar experience.

6. IMPROVED WEBSITES AND MOBILE PHONE STRATEGIES:

Businesses that are selling online products have also started working on strategies that they can use to make the user experience better and enhanced. They have constantly been updating and adding new features to their websites for both the website and mobile phone interfaces. Doing so has made it very easy for the customers to have a smooth and easy experience. They can find products on their websites pretty easily as the user interfaces are no longer complex. Finding the perfect is not an issue any longer, it could be done very easily. Filters have been introduced to the websites. These filters help you to filter out the product you need out of the whole stock. Products can be filtered out on the basis of product categories, price ranges, etc. Products can also be filtered out and searched for by their codes. If you know the product for the code, you can very easily retrieve the product that you need. These filters and other features that these online business owners have added to their websites have greatly helped the customers in finding their desired product without wasting much of their time. These efforts are all made, so the connection which these businesses have with their customers remains intact even through these uncertain times.

7. **CUSTOMIZATION:**

Online brands now offer customization too. Customers are facilitated by allowing them to customize their products as per their needs or will. For example, if there is a clothing brand and it allows customization, more people will be attracted to it because they will be able to make changes to the piece of clothing they show interest in and want to buy. They would be able to change the color of the dress as per their liking or change some design which they might not like. This customization makes the customers feel like they are being heard and that the brands are taking care and paying attention to their likes and dislikes. This has also helped to strengthen and maintain the relationship between the brands and their customers.

8. ASKING FOR FEEDBACK:

Asking for feedback from the customers is really important. This would allow you to identify your weak points. You always have to make sure that you cater to the needs of your customers and work as per their demand and liking. Most of the brands have adopted this technique in order to improve their services. Asking for feedback allows them to work on their negative points. By doing so, they are able to retain their customers as well and also strengthen their connection with them which nowadays in this virtual dealing a very important aspect that cannot be ignored. They can retain their customers by improving themselves in areas where their customers may have issues. Customers also should provide the brands with constructive and honest feedback. This is considered a step that the customers take to strengthen their virtual connection with the brand. If a brand overcomes a drawback that a customer may have highlighted, the customers also feel valued. They feel like their concerns are being heard, and attention is paid to their concerns.

9. ENGAGING CUSTOMERS WITH FUN ACTIVITIES:

Many brands have launched different fun challenges and activities that people can do by staying inside their homes. Multiple challenges have gone viral over the past few months on social media platforms like Tiktok and Instagram. The basic purpose of these challenges is in favor of both the businesses and the customers. The customers can help divert their minds from the constant anxiety and panic they feel, it is a marketing strategy for the businesses. These fun challenges and activities are being launched with the intention of getting viral. When these challenges go viral across the internet; this provides the brands and businesses with a lot of exposure. People get to know about them through these viral challenges. It is a kind of marketing strategy of them for their brand, and people take part in those challenges so they can forget the environment they are living in and the panicked situation they are in for a little while. Doing something which makes you happy is not going to cost anybody a thing.

10. GIVEAWAYS:

Brands have also started to launch giveaways. These giveaways are also a strategy to increase the reach of their brands. Giveaways are announced by the brands for their customers so they can take part in them and help the brand grow and in return, get a gift from their side as a token of appreciation. The basic purpose behind the giveaways is that they help the brand target more customers. They ask their followers to recommend their pages and brands to their friends and family to help with engagement with the brand. These giveaways really help the brand in maintaining and strengthening the connection with their customers. They appreciate the customers for their loyalty and for putting their trust in them. Giveaways are a gesture of being thankful from the brands to their customers. The customers, because of these kinds of gestures, feel appreciated and special. So they try even harder to help the brands with increasing their outreach and exposure. Giveaways were commonly seen by these online brands during the past months when the coronavirus brought the world to a halt. Brands also announce these types of giveaways on special occasions like new year occasions, Christmas, anniversaries of the brands or the businesses, and other such occasions. Brands realize the importance of their customers and thus, every once in a while keep announcing such giveaways for their customers, thus strengthening and maintaining their virtual connection even more.

These are just a few ways on how the brands have been working to improve their connection with their customers. Just as everybody nowadays is connected to others virtually, so are these brands trying to keep up with these virtual connections. These virtual connections are not only beneficial for them but also for the customers. Nowadays, brands have really started to focus on this aspect in order to improve their sales and retain their customers. If the customers start to feel that they are no longer special to these brands, they sway away to other brands that may give them more attention. If they are given more attention at some other brand they are never going to come back to you. You would lose a customer and your competitors would get one. Thus, such ways need to be adopted, so the customers stay loyal to these brands and the brands also do not lose their customers to their competitors.

CHAPTER 6

Impact Of Covid-19 On E-Commerce Industry

The pandemic in 2020 has completely changed the world. Nothing is the same as it was a year and a half back. The world now is living in constant fear due to the spread of novel coronavirus. Governments have imposed lockdowns and asked people to self-quarantine so as to curb the spread of this deadly virus. A lot of people have knocked at death doors because of this virus. Shops and markets have been closed down all across the world due to the lockdown situation. A lot of businesses have had negative impact on their sales because of the lockdowns, but they were required and were a necessary step to help in avoiding human contact and slow down the spread of the virus, if not completely stopping it. Different precautionary measures were issued by the World Health Organization which are a great help in controlling the spread of the virus. All this seemed abnormal a few years back but now it is the new normal and the world seemed to have become accustomed to it. This is something with which we have to live for some time.

Multiple industries have faced a situation of crisis after the spread of coronavirus as lockdowns were imposed, people lived in constant fear. They also had to make sure that they are maintaining social distance and thus preferred staying indoors. All the businesses were halted, their production slowed down up to a great extent. When the other industries had been going through these tough times, the e-commerce industry saw a new rise. The reason why this happened was that people could not leave their houses and were locked inside, due to which they had no other option left but to shop online. People started to order the basic necessities, food, beverages, clothes, home goods, baby stuff, animal goods, and basically each and everything that could help them spend a comfortable time while they are staying indoors. People preferred online shopping due to the rising anxiety and panic inside them due to the conditions of the outside world. Some people suffering from the virus showed mild to no symptoms, and you could not really tell who is infected and who not. Another reason that further pushed people towards online shopping was the increased use of the internet. Not just the use but the steady availability of the internet is also a great reason behind the rise in sales of e-commerce businesses. People wouldn't really have anything productive to do and they would end up using internet a lot which resulted in the trend of increased online shopping. Covid-19 has had a great impact on the e-commerce industry. The sales have been skyrocketing ever since the lockdown started. Here are a few ways how covid-19 had been a positive impact on the e-commerce industry.

1. **ONLINE PROFIT MARGIN:**

    The pandemic has been a reason for the disrupted supply chains in all businesses. Customer service has also been poorly affected, but the fact that online business owners have generated great revenues, and their sales have increased a lot. They also have had an online profit margin of 38 percent. Many people have seen profits as their sales have skyrocketed due to the increase in online shopping in a global pandemic. Almost 40 percent of business owners have claimed that they have generated great profits during the pandemic. Although a little fraction of business owners say that they have seen a decline in their sales and profits due to the global pandemic. Fifteen percent of the business owners have claimed that their sales decreased as a result of covid-19.

2. **WORKFORCE ADJUSTMENT:**

    Due to the global pandemic, many companies have had workforce adjustments. Companies brought made changes in their workforce. Around 44 percent of the companies had to relocate the staff because of the covid-19. Most of the companies have hired new employees due to an increase in sales of their business. Also, some of the business owners had to face the situation where they had to fire their employees because of the decrease in sales of their businesses. Some of the companies, due to the increase in their sales, ended up increasing their salaries.

This increase in salaries of the employees came as a piece of good news to them because of the uncertainty in these situations of the covid-19 pandemic. Some of the companies have also reduced the salaries of their employees because they faced a decrease in their sales. Also, around 21 percent of the companies have announced that they made no changes and adjustments in their workforce. This came as a surprise because of the situation that the world is facing nowadays. These workforce adjustments were made keeping in view the sales and revenue increases of the businesses. Some adjustments were made according to the negative trend that was observed as a result of the covid-19 pandemic.

3. **OMNICHANNEL BUSINESSES:**

The businesses that have both online stores and physical stores are called omnichannel businesses. An interesting fact was revealed about these Omnichannel business owners that 23 percent of their sales increased in the physical stores while 16 percent of the business owners stated that their sales did not get affected and stayed the same. As for 43 percent of the companies, their offline sales took a hit.

4. **INTRODUCTION OF NEW TRENDS:**

Due to the lockdown situation, uncertainty constantly lingers around and this panic persists, many businesses feared going out of business. In order to avoid those situations, they introduced new concepts and new trends in their businesses in order to stay relevant. The businesses that introduced new trends in their businesses saw a great rise in their sales because they were providing people the convenience that they needed. They made sure that the overall shopping experience of the people gets improved. Many stores introduced free delivery services. Some of the stores that did not offer any delivery services before now offered these services. Some of them made sure that the delivery of items purchased in as fast as possible so that the parcels reaches out in time to their respective buyers. Introduction to the new trends in their businesses turned out to be a good and positive idea for the success in their businesses.

5. **ESSENTIAL SERVICES SAW A RISE IN SALES:**

The stores that were selling the essential services saw a great rise in their sales. The stores which deal with providing the stuff that is necessary for survival have had their sales improved. People bought the items like toilet paper, food items, sanitary products, and other such stuff that is required and essential. These items were also seen in shortage. Soaps, hand washes, sanitizers, and toilet papers were also reported to have been out of stock. The companies after seeing this situation, increased their production speed so that all these items reach out to people in time and are always readily available so that the people do not panic. In such uncertain and hard times, mass panic is very important to be avoided.

6. SOCIAL DISTANCING:

One of the basic safety precautions issued by the World Health Organization is to maintain a distance of almost 6 feet from other individuals in order to protect yourself from the coronavirus. Coronavirus is can be spread through the air and can easily transmit from one person to another if someone coughs or sneezes in close proximity to you. The health experts encouraged everyone to be at a distance of at least 6 feet from one another in order to slow the spread of covid-19. Almost 52% percent of the customers are practicing social distancing and thus avoid going to the markets physically. Although, the superstores and other markets have made sure that the customers are able to maintain follow all the precautionary measures and maintain their safe distance from one another. But still it is better to avoid going to the markets and stay at home. Also, in the lockdowns and self-quarantine situations, the only possible option for a person is to shop online. Due to the reason for practicing social distancing, many online sellers and businesses have seen a rise in their sales. Online shopping is convenient as well as it is safe. You don't have to leave your house and go to the markets but instead, you can receive everything that you need right at your doorstep without any hassle.

7. PURCHASE OF MASKS, SANITIZERS, GLOVES INCREASED:

Masks, sanitizers, gloves, and all those things that help you in slowing down the spread of the covid-19 were purchased excessively by people. Many people started their own little businesses out of it. They would buy the masks wholesale and then sell them to people online. The excessive purchase of these items helped online businesses increase their sales up to a great extent. Most of the businesses flourished because these items were sold in bulk and in a great amount to the people. And due to the social distancing and stay-at-home orders, the customers would purchase these necessities from online businesses and sellers. An increase in the purchase of plastic and disposable gloves was also observed. These things were not only required to the common public but also the health care staff who are working hard all day and night to ensure that everybody heals from the chaos that this coronavirus has been causing.

8. **CUSTOMER FEEDBACK:**

Customer feedback has also been an important factor in increasing the sales of online businesses. Many businesses, both online and physical businesses, rely on customer feedback. This is very important for the growth and success of the business. This is a very way in which businesses can overcome their shortcomings. If the customers come across any unpleasant experience with the business while shopping, they post negative feedback. After posting the negative feedback, the businesses work on that aspect and try to make it better, so no other customer has to go through any unpleasant situation again. These customer reviews are very helpful for the businesses, and the businesses give them high importance because they want their business to grow large and not have stunted growth. The businesses, after improving the situation for future customers as well as existing ones reach out to their customers and let them know that they have overcome their drawbacks and shortcomings and that they do not find themselves in the same situation anytime again. This way, they are able to gain the trust of their customers. They keep coming back to these businesses and brands. Not just that, but they also spread the word and share about their experience and then the customer care services that have made an exemplary improvement. This also proves to be very helpful in attracting more customers. This is one of the very important ways due to which the business owners have seen great rises in their businesses. Also, in these uncertain times, the business owners are mindful of the fact that how they need to improve their customer services, retain the existing customers and attract more customers. They keep on improving their services, so they are preferred by their customers.

9. DEMAND IN INCREASED MEDICAL SUPPLIES:

Due to the covid-19 pandemic, the health care systems in many countries have collapsed due to the high number of covid-19 patients that are in critical condition and many of them on the death bed. Scarcity and inadequacy was observed with medical supplies. Not just the medical supplies, but many under-developed countries have also faced a shortage of medical officers and doctors. People have started to shop for the medical supplies online as well because the demand for these supplies increased a lot. Most of these medical supplies have been purchased online in order to maintain the covid-19 safety protocols. These medical supplies also have spiked sales due to online shopping and thus giving the e-commerce industry a boost. The sales have been greatly increased because the situation of the covid-19 is bad all across the globe. All the countries are struggling in order to reduce the active cases because of the covid-19 and also make sure that the people who are critically ill are treated well. The increase in ventilators has also been seen because of the increasing number of covid-19 patients in a critical state. In order to treat these patients, ventilators are required. Ventilators and other medical supplies that are in demand can also be purchased online without any hassle. PPE kits that are worn by the doctors are also in high demand so they can protect themselves as well. These health care workers have been working day in, day out in order to help the ones in need. And they can only do that if they are well themselves. Thus to ensure the safety and protection of these health care workers face shields, PPE kits have been in great demand and they have also boosted the businesses of online sellers. Medications and other administered drugs are also in great demand, and all of them are readily available to be purchased online. Online purchasing can help them avoid crowded areas and help protect themselves even more. Many medicine companies have seen a rise in their sales after the pandemic of covid-19 escalated. These are all the things that are essential for survival after getting affected by the covid-19. Let's suppose if a person has been affected by the coronavirus and wants to buy himself some medicines. If that person goes to a medical shop to buy those medicines, he will put a large number of people at risk as well. It would be better if that person purchases his medicines online and get them delivered to his house. This way he would be able to save a lot of people being at risk because of his state. Medicine companies have improved their websites and delivery services so that the buyers do not have to go through any inconvenience. Due to the increase in these medical supplies, relevant businesses and companies have seen their businesses touching new heights of success.

10. INCREASE IN SUBSCRIPTION SERVICES:

Due to the lockdowns and self-quarantining, many people have started to stay in their houses, so they are able to practice social distancing and avoid human contact as much as possible. Because of people staying in their houses, a great increase has been recorded in the subscription services of many platforms. Many streaming websites have seen a great rise in their sales and subscription services. Due to pandemic, people are staying inside their homes, and they need different forms of entertainment so they do not feel like they are caged inside their houses and have something to keep themselves busy with. The platforms that provide these services have also improved their businesses and customer care and support because they are mindful of the fact that they are needed and very much preferred by people in order to keep them occupied. These entertainment resources also help in the diversion of the state of mind. When a person starts watching movies or documentaries etc., they get busy with that, and their mind is automatically diverted from any stressful situation. Artists and the media industry have also been a major source of keeping people sane during these uncertain times and keeping them occupied as well. People resorted to these streaming platforms, and as a result their sales have spiked up and they have been doing really well.

DIFFERENT INDUSTRIES AFFECTED BY THE PANDEMIC:

Many industries have been affected by the pandemic, some negatively while others positively. The covid-19 pandemic had a great impact on the e-commerce industry due to the number of people staying inside their houses because of the coronavirus pandemic. People are ordered to stay indoors and only leave their houses in case of any emergency. People have started to prefer online shopping as going to physical stores is a risk and also because they have been shut down due to the lockdowns imposed in different areas.

Online stores that sell essential items have been doing great sales because people prefer to shop these products online rather than going to the stores. Foods, beverages, medical supplements, medicines like cough syrups, pain killers, masks, gloves, and other sanitary products have also been doing great sales ever since the coronavirus spread. After these basic essentials, other things that have been in great demand and people have been buying them a lot are categorized into a new category. As the ways of life have been greatly altered due to the pandemic, things that were not much needed by an ordinary man are now important because of the changes that covid-19 has brought in our lives. Life currently is becoming the new normal, and we have get used to this change in life as soon as we can. Some of the things that have been in great demand on the online retailing websites in this pandemic are stated below, let's have a look at them.

1. **OFFICE FURNITURE:**

   After the Covid-19 pandemic started to spread like wildfire, the offices encouraged people to stay at home. In order to keep the businesses running, employees were asked to work from their homes, due to which the sales of office furniture on these websites rose high. For people to work comfortably, they did need a proper office chair and a table. People started to purchase the office chairs and tables online and got them delivered to their houses, without any hassle of going to the furniture shops and exposing themselves to the infection.

2. **FITNESS SUPPLIES:**

   Gyms were closed down as well. The closing of gyms affected the people who were maintaining their fitness and following a fitness and exercise routine at the gyms. People could no longer go to the gyms and exercise there. In order to keep their health in check, they started to purchase these items online. People who did not go to gyms and stayed at home doing nothing, greatly destroyed their health. In order to stay healthy and fit they had to follow a fitness routine. The gym trainers would instruct people online, and they would do their exercises under the supervision of their instructors. Thus, the sales of the gym equipment and other fitness supplied increased a great deal on these online retail marketplaces.

3. **COSMETICS:**

Cosmetics and other products related to beauty also had a rise in their sales. These cosmetics and beauty products were used mostly by females. Many females also started to work on improving their makeup skills. So when they would run out of any product, they would purchase those products online. Also, many of the cosmetics companies put sales on their products in order to attract more customers, and this tactic surely worked. Many females ordered and bought cosmetics and other beauty products from these online retailers.

4. **TOYS:**

Kids had to be retained at home because of the spread of coronavirus. To keep the children busy and home and not let them go outside, parents preferred getting them new toys to engage them with new stuff so they learn and can have fun simultaneously. A lot of parents purchased toys for their kids online, and as a result, the sales of toys on these online websites also improved their sales.

5. **ENGAGING AND INFORMATIVE STUFF:**

Because of the lockdowns and self-quarantine, people started to spend more time indoors, and they obviously needed fun stuff to keep them occupied and busy in their free hours. The sales of stuff that helped the people kill their free time during lockdown and quarantine increased up to a great extent as well. People indulged in buying books and novels etc., to read in their free time. Many people started to develop new hobbies, and in order to engage themselves with their new hobbies, they purchased stuff accordingly. A lot of people developed the hobby of gardening during the quarantine and they started spending more time in their gardens, nurturing and taking care of the plants. If anybody did not have any garden in their house, they made one feel fulfilled. The increase in sales of such stuff was seen a lot as well.

6. HOME FURNISHING AND DECORATING:

A huge number of people started to renovate their houses. They decided to change the nooks and corners of their house to feel fresh. Also, they find something with which they can spend their free time. People started buying new furniture and other decorations for the renovation of their houses. This was commonly seen among those people who always need something to keep them busy. They used this as a way to spend their free time productively. Sometimes life gets so busy that you hardly get time for other stuff, now due to work from home and stay at home orders people had free time on their hands, and they indulged themselves in different healthy activities, home renovation and decorating among as well. Home furnishing and other stuff that is used to decorate houses was also commonly seen purchased by people, thus increasing their sales a lot.

7. EDUCATIONAL SUPPLIES:

Due to the closing of schools and other educational institutes, people started online studies. Teachers would conduct online classes. Due to online education, educational supplies were also in demand that people purchased from these online marketplaces because it is a safe option in such difficult and uncertain times. Sales of these products were also increased and as a result of the pandemic.

8. INTERNET AND MOBILE DATA:

Internet and mobile data have been the main source of keeping boredom at bay during this lockdown and quarantine situation. People have started to use their cell phones more than ever. A huge increase in the internet and mobile data services was seen. The sales of internet services have been soaring high ever since. The Internet provides a gateway to these people to the outer world that they are unable to because of the stay in home orders by the governments of different countries. People also have been accessing different entertainment stuff by internet and mobile data services. Internet and mobile data services have been keeping people updated about what is going on all around the world. Also, these services play a key role in providing them with the latest updates from their governments regarding the situation of the infected people and the coronavirus in their countries. Also because people have started to work from home, they need a stable and fast internet to do their work in its due time. Due to the reasons stated above, we can safely say that internet services have been greatly purchased by people and this is one of the most essential and important services for people.

9. **MOBILE PHONES AND LAPTOPS:**

Mobile phones and laptops have also recorded great sales during the pandemic. These devices are a need of the time nowadays. Everything has been digitalized and this is the basic requirement. If you are a student or an employee at some office, you do need these items in order to keep your affairs in order. The importance and use of these telecommunication devices have been increased multiple folds; people have been buying these things excessively because their uses have increased. Record sales of mobile phones and laptops have been seen ever since the coronavirus started to spread and restricted people to their houses. This has given e-commerce industries and companies a great boost.

These are some of the important essentials of the new way of living nowadays, and increased sales of these items have really given the e-commerce industry the boost it needed. While these industries saw a rise in their sales, some have seen their sales go down as well. A few of which are given below.

1. **LUXURY ITEMS**:

Sales of luxury items have seen a great decline in their sales ever since the pandemic gathered its momentum. People prefer to spend their money on the basic necessities of life rather than opting for luxury goods.

People stopped purchasing these items, and thus it has seen a drastic decrease in their sales. The economy has been greatly affected due to the spread of coronavirus and its rapid spread, and in such situations, nobody has the money to purchase luxury items.

2. TOURISM:

Due to the spread of covid-19, many countries have shut down with lockdowns imposed. Stay at home orders have been given to the people in order to contain the spread of the virus. Many countries have sealed their borders, and nobody is allowed to enter. Many airlines have their flights suspended because of the rising cases of coronavirus. Online sale of tickets has also seen a great decline because tourism has been greatly impacted. Not just the international travel has been banned by many countries, but the local tourist spots have also been shut down for the common public. This step of banning tourism both locally and internationally had been taken in order to slow down the spread of the virus as much as possible. It has been observed that ever since tourism has been banned, a decrease in the coronavirus positive has been seen. So we can say that the tourism industry may have been affected by these bans, but it has helped the situation a little.

3. FASHION INDUSTRY:

The fashion industry is yet another industry that has seen a great decline in its sales. Fashion weeks have been canceled due to these lockdowns and stay-at-home orders. You are not really able to practice social distancing in such gatherings, so they are avoided altogether.

Many industries have seen rise in their sales and their businesses flourishing during the pandemic, but others have been seeing drastic declines in their sales as a result of the pandemic. This is the new normal, and this is something with which we have to live our lives for some time now.

HOLIDAY SEASONS AND SHOPPING:

As countries have been going into lockdowns and enforcing strict rules in order to practice social distancing, people are unable to celebrate the holiday season as they had been doing in the past. Now due to the current situation, people prefer to do all their holiday shopping online rather than going to the stores. Businesses also have seen the preference of people towards online shopping has started to pay more attention to their online stores. As the cases have been rising, people are getting more and more inclined towards online shopping. The holiday season during 2018 saw a great rush in stores as people turned to the physical stores for their holiday season shopping, whereas in 2019 and onwards, it has been observed that people turn more towards apps and online websites for their holiday season shopping. These holiday seasons and online shopping have been a reason for the increase in sales of different online businesses and stores. People also turn towards these online shopping apps and websites because they provide you with convenience as well as safety. You do not have to leave your house and get yourself exposed to the coronavirus but would receive everything that you have purchased at your doorstep. According to statistics, it had been seen that shoppers preferred shopping early for the holiday season, so they do not have to go through any potential delay in delivering the products that were purchased. Due to the ongoing pandemic, a lot of businesses have been victims of the supply chain disruptions. Although, the businesses are working on this issue still to avoid any delay with delivery they placed their orders a little early.

Multiple research reports have been issued addressing the changes in the shopping behavior and pattern of the shoppers during the holiday season. A report states that many online retailers have seen record sales during the holiday season. It was seen that around 37 percent of the people preferred to shop and spend online as compared to the past years because they know the risks that come with shopping in the physical stores. Many giant e-commerce websites saw record sales during holiday seasons. Chinese websites Alibaba and JD.com set new records of sales during Singles Day in November the previous year. They racked up almost $115 billion in sales on these online websites. Such sales have never happened online ever before. In the first hour of the online sales, Southeast Asia's Lazada, which is a company owned by Alibaba, saw great sales of approximately $100 million. These have been recording sales for any company within an hour of a shopping event. This clearly shows how much people have been inclined towards shopping online due to the pandemic. Not just that, but the sales that happened during Black Friday and Cyber Monday have been touching new highs. Black Friday sales have been increased up to 22 percent and achieved a new record of $9 billion, which is a great number of single-day sales are concerned. Cyber Monday online sales have almost shot up to $10.8 billion. Cyber Monday sales have also been recorded as the largest U.S online shopping sales ever.

By observing the inclination of buyers towards online shopping during the holiday season, many businesses have started to invest in it because they know that this is the need of the time, and this is something that is preferred by the shoppers. They have now started to take these matters more seriously. They never really paid attention to these things before because they were not in common practice as they are today, and its importance is going to increase with every passing day. They are also making changes according to the needs and wants of the buyers and are getting themselves prepared for the surge of online shopping because a lot of buyers have transitioned from shopping at physical stores into shopping at online stores. The online businesses are not really prepared for this transition, but they are leaving no stone unturned in making the online shopping experiences of these shoppers better.

ONLINE PAYMENTS ARE PREFERRED:

Before the spread of the coronavirus, people favored paying for their items using the cash-on-delivery option because they were not really comfortable with the whole idea of paying online. But now, as the spread of the coronavirus has increased. People have started to pay for their online purchasing through online digital cards and avoid paying with the currency notes as in cash on delivery. This is also a trend that was commonly seen during the rise in sales of online shopping. Paying through digital cards is really helpful in boosting the digital economy.

PERSONALIZATION:

It has been observed that when the customers are given an option for personalization while shopping online, they tend to buy more. According to the statistics, customers spend 48 percent more when they are given the option of personalization by a business or a brand. Also, it has been observed that 57 percent of the people who shop online are willing and comfortable to share any personal information if that information makes their shopping experience better. Making the shopping experience of the buyers has to be the main priority of the business owners because if they did not have customers, they would not be able to make any profit. While making the shopping experience of the customers more personalized, it would make the customers think that they are appreciated and are listened alike. This would help in generating an emotional bond of trust and loyalty, then that customer would not go elsewhere to shop. This way, the brand or the business would be able to retain the customer and also help attract more customers. Thus, it is very important that the brands now pay attention to having a personalized shopping relationship with the customers. The businesses that have grown mostly in the past have practiced and implemented this strategy of providing and maintaining personalized relationships with their customers and clients.

BRANDS WITH CELEBRITY ENDORSEMENTS:

Those online businesses and brands that have been endorsed by celebrities have also seen a rise in their sales. These celebrities are massively followed by people and they often buy the products that are endorsed by them. Many famous celebrities and influencers with a huge fan following have been roped into promoting and endorsing the products a business is offering. This way, the brands are able to increase their reach to the potential customers. Brands have started to adopting these techniques so they can improve their sales even more in this pandemic situation where so many businesses have suffered greatly.

BETTER AND IMPROVED PRODUCT IMAGES:

Online shopping can be tricky for some people as they hesitate when they are about to press the purchase button because they are not very sure about the product they are about the purchase. If they see that the product they are so hesitant to buy has better quality and design, the hesitation is decreased a little, and they end up purchasing that product. This hesitation can be reduced and decreased up to a certain extent by adding good quality and improved images so the buyer can see the product clearly. Also, it is important that proper description is added to the products so that if any buyer has any questions that is stopping them from purchasing the product can be answered beforehand. Many online businesses have started following this practice, and the sales that they have been doing are touching the skies. These are all these little strategies that are very important in running businesses smoothly. Better use of technology has also been a great driving force in increasing the sales of different online brands and websites.

CONCLUSION:

Great sales have been seen due to these latest trends in technology that businesses are following. Covid-19 has greatly disrupted the normal lives of people, and this new normal way of life has been the reason for the increase in the sales of e-commerce companies and brands. People have started to live their lives according to the new norms of today's world due to the widespread coronavirus. They have understood the importance of social distancing and other safety precautions. They know that going to the markets and leaving their houses could expose them to great risks of the coronavirus. The risks would not only be affecting them but also the people they love and care about. Due to which they chose a safer and more convenient option of online shopping. Be it shopping for the daily essentials, necessities, or shopping during any holiday season; they prefer doing it all online. These online shoppers have played a great role in increasing the sales and profits of the online retailer marketplaces. The E-commerce industry has flourished and bloomed like no other industry during the pandemic.

Chapter 7

Covid-19 And Amazon Sellers

Covid-19 has had a great impact on the e-commerce industry. Many online businesses have seen their sales soar up when the pandemic hit the world hard. Many people resorted to doing online shopping to maintain the covid-19 safety protocols. Just so the virus do not spread a lot, lockdowns were imposed that further pushed people to continue shopping online. Marketplaces like Amazon, Alibaba, eBay etc. saw great rises in their sales. People turned towards online shopping not just for the basic necessities but also other essentials which they required while staying inside their houses. Holiday seasons also resulted in great sales because of people shopping in bulk. Amazon sellers have been doing really great. Let me discuss the impact that the covid-19 had on the businesses of these amazon sellers.

FULFILLMENT BY AMAZON (FBA) AND ITS IMPACT:

Amazon had invested a lot in their fulfillment by amazon or the FBA program. Amazon had seen great spikes in its sales after the pandemic happened. Many new customers started to purchase items online and in order to facilitate them. Amazon had started to make some big decisions so they are able to facilitate the customers and also have an impact on the sellers with their FBA program. The changes that have been with the FBA program are long-lasting. These have also affected consumer demand and the behavior of a consumer.

Gym equipment, office equipment, and other essential supplies have been in great demand. The sellers of amazon have been keeping a close eye on these essentials and trying to take full advantage of these supplies in demand.

IMPORTANT STATISTICS OF AMAZON:

Amazon presented some important statistics after covid-19 happened. People have started to buy online rather than going to the stores. Buying online has been a convenient and safe alternative. Also, after the lockdowns were imposed, many shops have been closed down.

1. According to the statistics presented by the Amazon sellers, it was shown that the demand of gloves, medical masks and respirators increased by 17000 percent. The sales for these items increased because they have been in great demand. Covid-19 has been putting people to go through serious health problems. Coronavirus damages lungs the most and disrupts the respiratory system of the victim. Due to this reason the demand of masks and respirators has increased.

2. Food items have always been in great demand but people mostly would get them from the physical stores. Covid-19 caused the purchasing of these items online as well. The sales of the food items on the amazon website increased by 47 percent. People avoided going to the stores to get these items and thus used these online marketplaces to purchase the things that they needed.

3. Home renovation and improvement supplies also presented a spike in their sales. The sales of these items also increased by 47 percent.

4. The health and safety items have also seen an increase in their sales over the Amazon marketplace. These items have increased their sales by 98 percent.

5. Fitness supplies were also seen frequently purchased by people. Their demand increased 86 to 160 percent.

6. In short, we can say that health products have been in very high demand. People bought them in bulk which made Amazon run out of these health and safety products. As covid-19 is a health hazard. That is why these products were frequently purchased by people from these online marketplaces. They did so because going to physical stores meant exposing themselves to extra risks.

CUSTOMER DEMAND:

The customer demand for different products has increased during the pandemic and the marketplaces, Amazon being one of them has been continuously trying to fulfill the demands and needs of its customers in the pandemic when most of the people are turning towards these online marketplaces for purchasing the basic necessities of life.

The sellers try their best to keep every little thing in check so whenever the customer places an order for anything that they need all those items are readily available and not out of stock.

SHIPPING RESTRICTIONS:

The Fulfillment by Amazon program also had shipping restrictions on what items were to be sent into the warehouse. This step of restriction was taken as a precautionary measure in order to slow down the spread of the coronavirus. Also because of the fact that the demand of the customers increased with time and current situations. Those items were shipped to the warehouses that were in great demand by the customers. This was done so that the essential items that are frequently purchased by the people are always in stock.

CATEGORIES THAT WERE PERMITTED DURING THE FBA RESTRICTIONS:

Some of the categories that were permitted during the restrictions by Fulfillment by Amazon program are given below:

- Health Supplies

- Household Supplies

- Baby Products

- Personal care and hygiene products

- Food and groceries

As the sales of sellers increased on the online marketplaces, many new sellers came into business and launched their products on Amazon. More people turned towards these online marketplaces and it totally makes sense that even after the pandemic is over people will utilize these online platforms for shopping as they are more convenient and safe.

SUSPENSION OF SHIPMENT OF NON-ESSENTIAL GOODS:

The products which do not belong to any category as given above, are all categorized as non-essential goods. This has disrupted the businesses of few sellers. Like if there is a seller on Amazon that sells luxury goods and just because the Amazon fulfillment program is not allowing him to ship his products to the Amazon warehouse as they are considered non-essential. So, if anyone wants to buy any of the items which that specific seller selling, he would not be generating any profit because those will not be available at the Amazon warehouse. This would result in increased shipment costs and delay in shipping deliveries to potential customers. This has affected a few businesses because they may not be essential but some people may end up buying those products. This suspension of shipment of the Fulfillment by Amazon has affected the sales of the items that Amazon deems unimportant or non-essential. They have focused more on the essential items and those which were high in demand by the customers. These items have spiked their sales up to a great extent.

REASONS TO WHY YOU SHOULD GET STARTED WITH FULFILLMENT BY AMAZON PROGRAM:

Fulfillment by Amazon program is a great initiative launched by Amazon for their sellers. This is a great time for the new sellers who want to start their business with Amazon. Almost half of the products that are sold online are done by Amazon so it is a great way to start any new business on Amazon as a seller. Fulfillment by the Amazon program can benefit you in many ways. One of them being, you do not have to worry about any customer service or fulfillment even if you are running a business of physical products. Fulfillment by Amazon program has covered that aspect for you. The Covid-19 pandemic has been a cause for the downhill journey of many businesses but the e-commerce industry has taken some giant steps towards making great sales and generating profits. They have been taking extra steps in order to make the business experience for their third-party sellers more smooth and comfortable. These third-party sellers have been doing great for themselves by sitting at their homes and generating great profits. All the new sellers need to hop into all this and make use of this opportunity, that way they would be able to maintain and follow the stay-at-home orders and also they would start with something that would help the customers meet their demands and also would be helpful for them to make great sales.

If you are one of them who is looking to start an online business with Amazon as a seller, it would be great if you start now because the e-commerce industry is blooming and flourishing with every passing day. You would be able to achieve much more by the Fulfillment by Amazon policy so without any further you should get started. Here are a few other reasons why it is the right time to avail of any such business opportunity.

1. **INCREASED DEMAND:**

As many countries have been going into strict lockdowns and stay-at-home orders by their local governments they are unable to visit any brick-and-mortar shops. That is why they are turning to these online marketplaces to meet their needs. Previously this practice was not so common but now after people transitioning more towards these online marketplaces like Amazon, e-commerce has started to regain the pace it once lost. The demands for different categories of products have been increasing ever since the pandemic started and people have been asked to stay at their houses. The difficulty that Amazon had faced before the covid-19 pandemic no longer exists as there have been breaking record sales happening after the pandemic and more people turning towards these online stores. Amazon previously struggled to meet the demands of physical products by its customers but that struggle is no more there as they have recruited around 100,000 workers and that is not enough. They are still planning to recruit at least 75000 more. Amazon has again started to accept products from different categories and started to place them in their warehouses. An increase in the demand for different essential products has been seen during the pandemic but also other products that are not essential have been seeing positive growth in their sales. You need to see what categories are being positively affected by the Covid-19 pandemic and who are hurting as a result. You can pay more focus on those categories and start to launch their products so you don't have to suffer in your business.

2. **GETTING THE HANG OF THE PROCESS IS TRICKY:**

The journey of selling products on Amazon could be a little tricky and challenging at first and you could possible problems but once you get the hang of it you would be able to do it in no time and make the most out of it. You should start now so as time progresses and the pace of the sales increase you are able to make the most profit out of those sales. There are a few steps that would help you with your journey of selling products on Amazon. You need to look into details so you don't end up making mistakes and committing blunders. Now that Covid-19 has allowed us some free time at home, that is something which we have to take full advantage of. You can start watching different tutorials, read relevant articles or talk to a seller on Amazon to help you with the process. Learn about everything and time is something which you should not let slip out of your hands. There are free courses which you can start so you are able to learn about the whole process in detail and get aware of everything.

3. STABILIZATION OF SUPPLY CHAIN:

The sellers on Amazon previously had to go through the disruptions that were caused in businesses due to the supply chain. Products that were in high demand by the common public ran out of stock and could not be restocked because China was in strict lockdown. The situation worsened in China with every passing day making it difficult for the online sellers to arrange the products as they were not manufactured. The majority of the third-party sellers of Amazon are located in China. Now that situation in China has gotten better and the country is out of the strict lockdown and stay-at-home orders they are back into the business. The country is slowly and gradually coming back to normal. They have restarted manufacturing and also many of the factories have started working overtime in order to meet the demands of the common public. This has resulted in the stabilization of the supply chain disruptions that have been a huge problem for the Amazon sellers.

Selection of the products that you would want to manufacture is also very important to be remembered. You can start with those products that are high in demand and have low competition. This is a crucial step in the whole process. After you are able to decide on what products you would want to manufacture, you need to start looking for a reliable manufacturer who can manufacture those products for you. You need to look for those manufacturers that are functioning completely so you are able to bring your product to life. For manufacturing purposes, you can reach out to the suppliers available at Alibaba.

INCREASE IN AMAZON VISITORS:

The lockdowns and the quarantine situations are keeping people inside their houses. They do not have anywhere else to go as everything has been shut down by the local governments in order to slow down the spread of the coronavirus. People have started to spend more time on their phones and this has resulted in a great increase in Amazon visitors. People have started to shop online as it is both convenient and safe during such uncertain and tough times. Also, people have started to just go through the sites even if they do not have to buy anything specific. They just open the site and see what is on it and what they could possibly need. This is a kind of window shopping over these online marketplaces. Amazon and other such companies have made the whole shopping experience of their customers very comfortable and easy, that is why people do end up buying more than they need or buy stuff that they do not even need. This has led people to buy impulsively. Customers have started flocking the Amazon website as the brick-and-mortar shops have been closed down. From March 14 to March 17, the number of daily visitors on Amazon rose from 5-18 Million up to 73.55 Million people daily. These were the statistics from the year 2020. If you compare these stats with the previous year you would see that during the same time last year these stats were stable and no such increase was seen. The visitors on Amazon from March 14 to March 17, 2019, were around 68 million. Across all the brands, the sales of Amazon grew by 20 percent at the beginning of March 2020. Their sales increased by more than they had planned or thought of in the non-essential categories. Whereas, the sales of Amazon increased by 100 percent in the essential category products. At the beginning of March 2020, the most searched item was toilet paper. This product was in the first place for quite some time. The first 50 products in the search list were all from the essential categories. They were mostly the personal care and hygiene, household items, sanitizers, medical masks, and stuff like that.

PROFIT GENERATED BY AMAZON SELLERS DURING THE COVID-19 PANDEMIC:

Around 85 percent of the Amazon sellers have stated that they have generated enough profit in the year 2020 and will be going in the year 2021 as profitable. They have made a profit that would last till the year 2021. Their sales greatly increased and spiked high during the pandemic. This pandemic turned out to be a blessing in disguise for most of the sellers on Amazon and other such online marketplaces. Almost 62 percent stated that their profits have increased during the year 2020 as compared to their profits generated in the previous years.

EXPANSION OF BUSINESSES:

Due to the profits generated during the pandemic, many of the sellers on Amazon have started to plan the expansion of their businesses. Around 96 percent of the Amazon business sellers are thinking of expanding their businesses as they have seen huge profits in the year 2020. Expansion of their businesses has become one of the top priorities of the Amazon sellers. Many of the sellers have started to think about selling their businesses on Walmart.com and instead move to Shopify, Instagram, and other such platforms in the year 2021.

NEW SELLERS ON AMAZON:

As the sales spike on Amazon and businesses have started to generate profits during the pandemic due to the transition of people towards online shopping. It has started to attract more and more sellers to start their businesses on Amazon. The sales that have been happening on Amazon during the pandemic have been enormous. Many sellers have been able to generate enough profit for them to expand their existing businesses. Many new sellers have started their businesses now but they are facing the problems of increased prices of ads on Amazon. Almost 62 percent of the sellers are concerned about these increased prices of ads on Amazon. Also, the competition among sellers is now very tough among sellers because there is an increased number of sellers on Amazon and their competition has resulted in the driving of the product prices down.

HIGH PRICES OF PRODUCTS:

Prices of different products have also increased due to the ongoing pandemic. Due to the pandemic, many people have started to divert to online shopping and prefer it more as compared to shopping from brick-and-mortar shops. Demands for the essential goods have increased. Demand has increased because people have started purchasing these items more frequently. This has resulted in running different products out of stock. Amazon sellers were not ready for all this to happen and also because shipping to the Amazon warehouses was suspended for the items that were categorized as non-essential items. Due to the products going out of stock and also because of the suspension of shipping products to the Amazon warehouse, prices of different prices were increased by the sellers. The prices were also increased due to another reason. The sellers wanted to make more profit because they clearly understood what items were in more demand by the people and would end up buying them no matter what. Prices were increased as a result. Many sellers on Amazon also generated profits by increasing the prices of different products that were high in demand by the common public. Around 13 percent of the sellers priced their products high to the challenges that were faced due to the spread of the coronavirus.

PROFITS GENERATED BY THE AMAZON SELLERS:

Just because the sellers knew that what products were in demand, in order to generate more profit out of that they tried to sell that product more. An example of this could be that they knew toilet papers and other health care supplies have been in great demand so in order to generate more profit they focused more on selling those products. Around 14 percent of Amazon sellers were such who started to sell those products that were in demand. The sellers that have had an experience of a year or two, these sellers are considered as new sellers as they do not have a lot of experience were able to generate a profit of $42,000 per year. If the new sellers were able to generate this much profit you can clearly imagine how much profit would be the experienced sellers generating. The percentage of profit they would be generating is evident. The benefits which these online sellers have generated from people shifting to online shopping are much. The economies of different countries were plagued because of the coronavirus but the online sellers benefitted greatly from this transition of people.

PROBLEMS FACED BY THESE SELLERS AND HOW TO OVERCOME THESE THEM:

While many sellers benefitted from the spiked sales on Amazon and other such marketplaces, they also faced problems. Different problems that they encountered and how could they be easily combatted are explained below:

1. **FULFILLMENT BY MERCHANT (FBM):**

    Fulfillment by Merchant or FBM is something that the sellers can try when Amazon freezes the shipments. Rather than sitting helplessly not able to do anything, Fulfillment by Merchant can provide them some way to keep making sales and generating profit as well. Many sellers have been trying Fulfillment by Merchant as Amazon warehouses are only used for the shipment of the products from the essential categories. You should try to fulfill your products on your own rather than feeling trapped and unable to do anything for your business and try to find a storage area, if you have one just utilize that.

This would also give you the advantage of the buy box. Nowadays Amazon has been favoring the Fulfillment by Merchant sellers and how they are making efforts into making both ends meet. They are also favoring them for the efforts they are making for being placed in the buy box.

2. **DECREASE YOUR COSTS:**

The times are tough and you never know when you have to go through a harsh time in your business. If you are making sales now and are able to generate profits currently try to save them for the future because you never know what kind of circumstances you have to face in the future. Nobody knows how long is all this going to last so it is better to reduce your extra costs and decrease your expenditure. This would help you a lot in the future. It is always wise to think and make some savings so the future gets secured. You should not spend everything ion the present. Nobody knows what the future holds. Do not overspend on the advertisements because now is the time people are spending on the essential items and you do not create a lot of advertisements for those items, people would buy them anyway.

3. **COME UP WITH GOOD STRATEGIES FOR YOUR BUSINESS:**

You need to have very strong and good strategies for your business. Strong and good strategies are going to help you greatly in generating profits. You need to work a lot on coming up with better strategies for running your business. Having only a single strategy is not a good practice. You need to have more than one strategy for your business. You need to have more than one strategy because circumstances and situations change and they never stay the same. You cannot apply one strategy to all the situations so you need to have more than one. So when it is time you can change it and help your business prosper. Even if you are a seller at Amazon you need to have strategies prepared on how you would be running your business. As the trends evolve, so should your business strategies. You have to make changes to your business strategies because if you do not do that you would become irrelevant. That is why it is highly important to have better and strong strategies beforehand for your business.

4. KEEP UPDATING YOUR INVENTORY:

You should always have your inventories updated so you don't end up running out of stock. Now in the current situation, you know what are products in great demand. You can try to produce as many such products as you can. This is very important if you are a seller because the number of sellers on Amazon has increased up a lot thus increasing the competition among different sellers. Many new sellers have joined Amazon as sellers after they have understood the situation and how they can benefit from this situation. After these new sellers, you need to be very vigilant and keep a close eye on your inventory so you don't run out of stock. If you do not have any product available, that would eventually give that sale opportunity to your competitor and you would lose a customer that is something that nobody wants. Keep updating your inventory with all products that you evaluate are in demand and frequently bought by people.

5. **KEEP YOURSELF UPDATED:**

As much as you need to keep your inventory updated so you do not lose any sales opportunity or a potential client you also need to keep yourself updated. You should know about all the relevant trends that are liked by people. You should have knowledge about all the things that people are most interested in nowadays. That would really help you in increasing your sales and in turn growing your business. You should also keep yourself updated regarding Amazon so you don't end up ruining your business. Make yourself and your business both capable enough so you are able to adapt to any changes. If you are able to adapt to these changes you would never lag behind others. Keep an eye on all the relevant and latest trends that are popular among the customers and Amazon as well.

Chapter 8

A Trigger For The Turning Point Of E-Commerce

The pandemic of Covid-19 had been a trigger for the turning point in the e-commerce industry. Previously the sales of the e-commerce industry have not been really dramatic and unusual but as soon as the world got hit by the coronavirus and people were forced to stay inside their houses in order to contain the spread of the virus. More and more people turned towards the online marketplaces so they are able to escape going to the brick-and-mortar stores and expose themselves to great risks of getting infected from the virus by some other individual. Coronavirus is highly contagious and spreads very quickly from one person to another. So in order to protect themselves from the effects of this deadly virus, people started staying inside their homes. This way the whole concept of shopping online was very much promoted. People started purchasing every basic and essential thing online. Thus the e-commerce industry revived, made record sales and ended up generating a lot of profit. This was the trigger for the turning point of the e-commerce industry. The sales and the profits that have been generated as a result are dramatic. As the customers went digital with everything they wanted to buy and purchase online, the retail share of the e-commerce industry soared to new highs. In comparison to the year 2019, the year 2020 saw a new era of success for the digital or e-commerce industry. In the year 2019, the retail share of the e-commerce industry was 14 percent whereas, in the year 2020, it shot up to 20 percent. Great transformations were recorded and seen as the pandemic happened. This began a new digital revolution in the e-commerce industry. It was also stated that e-commerce is going to keep blooming as it is until the end of covid-19 and even after the world recovers from the covid-19, e-commerce is still more likely to stay here and people would still continue to purchase from these e-commerce marketplaces. This digital revolution introduced new ways of life towards people. People started to make changes to their daily lives in order to get used to this new normal that we have to live along with now. The government did not step back from taking any responsibility is helping people to adapt to this changed lifestyle. The business owners have also been working hard and making efforts in order to make the shopping experience of their customers better. The great shifts from the brick-and-mortar stores to these online stores have also played an important role in stabilizing the economies of different countries that have been suffering ever since the lockdowns were imposed and the shops had to shut down eventually. Due to the lockdowns, businesses collapsed, completely affecting the economic value of that country. These great sales that have been happening in the e-commerce industry have played an evident role in making the economic situation better and this is something that will be remembered for a long. Different e-commerce websites and stores all across the world have been doing really well. They have been reporting at least double sales from the same time period in the previous year. Some companies have been making sales almost 50 percent higher than that of the previous year when the pandemic did not happen.

Although it is being said that the covid-19 proved to be a trigger in the turning point of the e-commerce industry but in some underdeveloped countries, no such things have happened. There are many reasons as to why aren't they able to make use of this situation as by the other developed or developing countries. A few of them are the little to no understanding of the digital devices, lack of trust by the consumers in businesses s, high charges of the broadband services. As we know that the concept of e-commerce originated after the first devices were introduced for communication so from this we conclude that it is very important to have knowledge of these digital devices if you want your e-commerce industry to grow and prosper. It is the duty of the governments to make their general public aware of the importance of these devices and how they play such an important role in our lives. If the common public is able to operate these digital devices, they would be able to make use of the e-commerce websites and purchase everything that they need with safety and convenience. It is also highly important that the consumers are able to put their trust in these online marketplaces. If the consumers are able to trust these businesses, they would purchase from them and that would play a crucial role in the growth of the e-commerce industry. If the consumers or the customers are able to trust the businesses they would become their loyal customers and shop from them, if they are unable to create that relationship of trust with their consumers they would not be able to become successful or make their business flourish. It is highly important to maintain that level of trust and loyalty with your customers so they keep comming back to you rather than going to your competitors. Internet is also a very important aspect when it comes to online shopping. You need to have a proper and stabilized internet connection to gain access to these marketplaces. In the countries where the broadband charges are high, there the people refrain from using any internet or spend their internet time over these online marketplaces. If you want your economy to become stable and grow during this pandemic you need to provide your people with proper internet so they engage themselves in purchasing from the online marketplaces and thus playing an important role in the stabilization of their country's economy.

Now you know that covid-19 had been a trigger for the turning point for the e-commerce industry, here are a few other ways to keep the current situation for as long as possible. Below are a number of ways that would prove helpful with making your e-commerce business even more successful after the turning point has occurred.

1. **OFFER SOMETHING FREE OF COST:**

   If you offer something free of cost that would be a great way to improve your business online. This is going to increase the sales a lot because who doesn't like free things, everyone does right? Suppose if you have a business where you offer subscription services and a person is not very familiar with what kind of products you are selling so that would make the unknown look scarier but if you offer a thirty-day free trial that is going to make it look less scary and also help your business. There would be no other obligations to follow, if the customer likes it he will subscribe again and then he has to pay the subscription charges. If he does not so he would cancel it there and then. If you are a business owner, you can offer something free among those. Like a fifty percent discount or get a free item if you purchase one. This would greatly help you in attracting more and more customers to your business.

2. **INCORPORATE A SENSE OF URGENCY:**

Sometimes the customers want to buy something but they need some time to think and during that time they sometimes forget what they were supposed to buy. This means you have lost a potential customer. In order to not lose that customer, you should incorporate a sense of urgency in your ads, etc. Write something like the sale of the discounts that you have been offering is about to end or is running out, this way the customers would not spend too much time to think if they want to buy the product or not. They would instantly buy so they do not lose the discounts you have been offering. It is a good tactic that can really help you in making extra sales and generating more profit.

3. MAKE YOUR CUSTOMERS CURIOUS:

Make complete use of the customer's curiosity. Do not fill them in with everything completely. If that information grabs their attention, they would want to have more of it and as a result, would contact you. Give your customers an itch that they must scratch so they get in touch with you and then you can talk about your business or products to them and help them convince themselves to buy the products you are selling. This is a great marketing gimmick that most businesses use.

1. **DISCOUNTS AND SALES:**

   If no other tactic or marketing strategy works, sales and discounts always does. Keep offering sales and discounts on your products so people can get attracted and buy your products. Nothing can attract the customers as the sales and discounts do. End of season sales, holiday sales etc. can greatly help you in leveraging your e-commerce business.

2. **MARKETING THROUGH INFLUENCERS:**

   Influencers have a great fan following. Hire these influencers and promote your products or business through them. Their reach is really going to help you improve your business a lot.

3. **SHOW STATISTICS:**

   If you are presenting statistics and show numbers that would help you in improving your credibility a lot.

This would make the customers feel that you are a reliable brand and they can trust you. Nowadays, a lot of fake brands have been scamming people online, which has reduced the trust people put in these online businesses. You can prove your credibility by presenting the correct statistics to convince them to buy from you. Also do not just fake numbers and statistics but use the real and proper ones so the customer does not consider you a scamming business.

4. **DISPLAY ENDORSEMENT:**

If you have some notable customers that endorse your products, do not forget to display those endorsements on your website. When people will know that you are backed up and supported by such prominent people, they would also want to buy from you. This is also a great way to display and show your credibility. The people who back you or support you should be related to the business you are promoting and the products you are selling. Give mentions of the top customers that use your products and endorse them. This provides a sense of authority and shows how much better you are than the others. This would help your business be distinguished from the others and would make it stand out among other such businesses.

5. **PROMOTE SIMPLICITY:**

Another thing that is going to make your business successful is trying out simpler ways. Do not make your order or purchasing process so complex that people do not buy from you. But instead make it simpler for them to understand. If they would know that they have to go through difficult and complex steps to purchase some product, they would run away from your website and most probably get it from somewhere where the process is not so complex. So you need to promote simplicity, it is going to give your business a boost and help you attract more customers. Promote your products with simplicity and also make the whole procedure of purchasing and placing orders simple so the customers end up buying from you. This is going to make the whole shopping experience fast, convenient, and effective. It is also in the human psyche that the brain tends to avoid complex situations and prefer simpler ones.

6. **STORY-TELLING:**

Telling your customers the stories and history of your business can also help create interest in your business. They would get curious about it and end up forming a connection with you. Some people are also interested in culture and heritage. These would be the ones taking more interest in your business. It is a good way to attract more customers towards your business.

7. **CLEAR AND IDENTIFY YOUR PURPOSE:**

Your business has a purpose; your business is your purpose. You should try to let your customers know what that purpose is. You need to identify what the purpose is. This is the mission behind your business.

You will only be able to prosper in your business if you know the purpose and mission behind your business. Many businesses are not able to flourish as they should have because they are not aware of their mission. This is because they lack a vision of how things are to be done. If you have a clear vision before you start your business that would greatly help you in identifying your purpose and help you in carrying your mission forward and do well for your business.

8. PROVISION OF A GREAT UI/UX BUSINESS:

If you are providing your users a good UI/UX experience, you are actually triggering their consciousness into getting attracted to your brand or business. It is a very good practice that can greatly help you in attracting more customers. You should have a responsive and interacting site or an app developed for your business. This would be a great help in taking your business forward. Provide your customers with ease and by using great UI/UX designs and experience. It is one of the most important ways that can help you in triggering the interest of customers towards your business. The pages should have relevant information and it should have ways that can help the customers easily filtering out the products that they need. The whole process of finding the product they want should be made easy, it is really going to help you doing great sales because the customer's user experience would not let them go anywhere else.

From this, we can conclude that covid-19 had been that triggering point where a new era of the revolution of e-commerce began. This revolution in the e-commerce sector was a long time coming still it took a pandemic for it to finally flourish and bloom like it should have. The increase in the sales and the profit that has been generated as a result of these sales has paved the way of helping the business owners who have businesses over these online websites to generate profits of the sales that have been happening and how people have turned to these online marketplaces ever since the pandemic happened. Covid-19 had played its part in diverting people's attention towards these online marketplaces. Now it is the job of these online business owners to make sure that they retain their customers and keep attracting them towards their businesses by giving them reasons. A few ways on how they can help their businesses not lose customers and retain them have been shared below. These ways can greatly help you with increasing the sales of your online businesses over these marketplaces.

Chapter 9

Growing Importance Of E-Commerce In A Post-Covid World

E-commerce has seen new heights of success during the ongoing pandemic all across the globe. People have been buying and purchasing stuff online. The sales of all the online marketplaces have increased up to a great extent. Online shopping provides customers with convenience and safety. This trend of online shopping was not commonly seen before, but as the pandemic happened and people started staying inside their houses because of the lockdown situation, many people turned towards online shopping. Online shopping has been a common trend ever since covid-19 happened and it is here to stay. The reliance of people on online shopping has increased its importance among the common public. Not just that its importance is going to keep growing even if the world is recovering from the coronavirus. This trend of e-commerce is here to stay. Currently, the governments have been easing the lockdowns but still, there is uncertainty looming around and no one knows what the future holds. People have been embracing Amazon and other such e-commerce marketplaces and also have gotten the hang of it and now there is no going back. That is because they find it extremely convenient and easy as compared to shopping from a brick-and-mortar store. In April 2020, the online shopping industry generated a revenue of 68 percent. This shows that this trend would still be very much in practice in comparison to the physical retailer shops.

FACTORS THAT WILL DRIVE THE E-COMMERCE GROWTH IN A POST-COVID WORLD:

Customers have been shopping online ever since the pandemic happened and they are most likely to keep shopping online when the covid-19 would end because of the following factors.

1. **THE CHANGE IN SHOPPING HABITS OF CUSTOMERS:**

   Since the inception of Covid-19, the shopping habits of people have changed drastically. They are relying moreover on these online websites and marketplaces to shop online. They have been shopping from the comfort of their houses. They are not going to leave this addictive habit of shopping and purchasing stuff online. When the retailer brick-and-mortar shops would open people would eventually move towards them, still it would take the time to move back from the convenient and easy way of shopping to shopping at the retailer shops. Things are now slowly and gradually going back to how they were before but the shopping habits of people have changed and are no longer the same. Covid-19 and the changed lifestyle that people adopted has also changed the shopping habits of people. People turned more towards the online marketplaces to shop for their daily essentials and products because of the increasing risk of the covid-19. Also, because of the lockdown situation that has restricted the common public to their houses.

2. **THE FEAR OF CATCHING THE CORONAVIRUS:**

Even if the world is going back to normal, the fears of catching the coronavirus are not going to disappear all of sudden overnight. People still have to take care of themselves and the people they love. It has been a deadly virus and has destroyed the lives of many people. It affects your health in a very negative way. Going to the brick-and-mortar shops means exposing yourself to great risks of catching a virus. In order to ensure protection against the coronavirus, people would still prefer to shop from these online marketplaces.

3. **INCREASE IN THE USE OF MOBILE DEVICES:**

Mobile devices have made the whole concept of online shopping very easy for the common public. Everybody now has a mobile device in their hands which is easier for them to use for the sake of online shopping. The increased use of the mobile devices has also played a very important role in people turning towards online marketplaces for shopping. There is no decrease in the use of these devices hence no decrease in online shopping from these marketplaces.

4. **STOCK OF ITEMS AVAILABLE IS A LOT:**

There had been cases reported where the items in the brick-and-mortar stores went out of stock when they were in great demand. The online stores give you the leverage of having these items delivered to your doorstep by ordering them in advance online. This helps you deal with the out-of-stock situations of different items. The online stock is enough and even if the business owners feel that they may run out of stock, they can very easily give orders for more production of the items. This is a very important aspect of online shopping. You can very easily get stuff delivered at your houses with no hassle at all and also with no fear that they would run out of stock. Even if they do you can always order in advance. Statistics can also play an important role here; it will let you know what product is in demand, what do you have enough, what else is that you need. Better statistical analysis would help you with overcoming issues that you face regarding the stock of your products available.

5. **HUGE VARIETIES OF STUFF:**

Variety is diverse while shopping online. If you want to purchase a product and you search for it, you will get to know how much variety is available. If one company has run out of that specific item that you need you can always get them from another one. It is a great way of getting stuff online as compared to brick-and-mortar stores. You do not have to keep waiting if a product is no longer in stock. You can always get it from the other stores that are doing business on the same marketplace or website.

6. CONVENIENCE OF SHOPPING:

Convenience is the most important advantage of online shopping. Online shopping comes with great convenience. You can buy anything you want to without having to leave your bed, let alone your house. You would just go to the online stores and click whatever you want to add to your cart. This is one of the main reasons why people would continue to shop online from these e-commerce marketplaces and how their demand would keep increasing even after the world goes back to normal.

These are some of the reasons that show that the trend of online shopping is going to increase exponentially in the future too. This change that has been brought into our lives will persist even after the world gets back to how it was before and the brick-and-mortar stores would start reopening. Just because of the increased change in these online shopping methods, many of the brick-and-mortar stores have shifted their businesses to e-commerce websites. The lockdown situations have greatly disrupted their normal business routines so in order to keep up with sales and not letting their businesses suffer they also shifted their businesses to the online marketplaces.

OMNICHANNEL STRATEGIES AND ITS IMPORTANCE:

Omnichannel marketing has many advantages. The customers have really appreciated the marketing strategies that these businesses have applied in order to facilitate them, these Omnichannel strategies have gained huge importance in the e-commerce industry. Merging the online shopping models and live shopping have greatly helped the customers. This is also easy for the customers to shop from their favorite brands or business even if their live stores are shut down. This would also help the businesses because if the customers are loyal to their brick-and-mortar stores, they would also shop from their online stores. This is valuable for the businesses and customers alike. The customers would be happy that even during the lockdowns and shutting down of the brick-and-mortar stores, their favorite brands or businesses are only a click away. Many Omnichannel stores have seen great sales happening due to their Omnichannel strategies. Many businesses are trying their best to find creative ways on how they can merge their online business and offline businesses together. Amazon is an online store, but it has also tried to work on the idea of physical or brick-and-mortar stores. They have opened a few physical stores at multiple locations in the United States of America. They have seen great sales happening on their online store but now they are trying new things and have started the chain of brick-and-mortar retail shops because they know that their customers would not disappoint them. Amazon is considered a giant online retail shop whose sales have been doubled in the past year.

Alibaba is considered the Chinese version of Amazon. It has also started to join the brick-and-mortar retail and opened up many shops throughout the country. They have been doing great sales not just online but in their offline stores as well. This depicts the importance of having better strategies in order to increase your presence. A great way is to merge the online and offline business. Walmart has also started working on improving its online presence. They have started to develop online stores where people are given an option to place orders and then go to the store only to pick the items that they ordered. This is a great way of doing shopping because they would not be waiting in long queues for their turns. Different online stores have started to venture into the idea of offline or brick-and-mortar stores and the brick-and-mortar stores have been seen transitioning and practicing their sales in the online marketplaces. Sephora is a large makeup brand; it has greatly evolved its business since it started. They have been working on the technology aspect where they allow their customers to see how the makeup treatments would look on them. This helps them to decide if they should buy the item or not.

Many brick-and-mortar stores have been trying to come up with different ways on how they can merge their offline store and online store together. Many brick-and-mortar stores have come up with convenient plans where they allow you to place the order online and then can visit the store to receive the order. This has been an easy way to avoid the long queues while placing orders. Many companies have also started working on their Omnichannel strategies. They had introduced apps where they can see what is available and what has run out of stock. It gives you all the relevant information that you need to know when you are shopping.

This has made it easy for them to shop. They would not be paying visits to the offline stores if the product that they need has run out of stock. These companies have started with the easy ways, then after completing their whole research they will eventually slowly and gradually move to better ways in order to make the shopping experience of their customers more comfortable and convenient.

SOCIAL MEDIA IS IMPORTANT!

Pandemic or no pandemic, social media promotion is very crucial and important for your business. Special attention needs to be paid towards social media marketing. Social media marketing can help you with increasing your sales up to a great extent. Social media marketing and promotion can take your businesses to new highs. It is something which the business owners need to take seriously and realize its importance as well. People have been using social media now more than ever and have started to pay attention to these business advertisements as well.

1. **SOCIAL MEDIA ADS FOR YOUR BUSINESS PROMOTION:**

    If you start to advertise your business on these social media platforms you will quickly see a great increase in your sales and customer outreach. You can invest in these social media ads on Facebook and Instagram etc. This would be a great boost for your business.

2. PINTEREST IS AN IMPORTANT TOOL FOR PROMOTION:

In order to promote your business well you can use Pinterest. Pinterest is a great tool that is going to help you expand your business. You can start uploading good quality pictures of your products on Pinterest and attract as many customers as you can. While using Pinterest for the promotion of your products make sure you post attractive pictures and make meaningful posts regarding your business. Announce your sales or discounts in creative manners. Make your customers feel curious about your brand or business. Use appropriate hashtags or the hashtags in trending, that would really help you increase the reach of your business or brand. Many people use Pinterest for inspiration you can make inspirational boards by adding the pictures of your products as pins. This would help you serve two purposes, it would help you advertise your business and it would also play an important role in providing organizational inspiration for people.

3. ENGAGEMENT WITH THE FOLLOWERS IS IMPORTANT:

Engaging and interacting with your customers or followers is very important. If you will interact with them and engage well with them they would develop a relationship or a connection with you and will keep on coming back to shop from you. If your customers are asking for something, answer their questions and queries. If they want to know about the price of some product, make sure you answer that question at that very moment so you do not lose your customers due to your laziness. Engage customers in fun challenges and also make sure you do some giveaways. Giveaways will help you kill two birds with a single stone. It would help you in appreciating your customers, your customers would feel loved and appreciated if you announce giveaways once in a while. Another important advantage that these giveaways have is that they help you in increasing your reach. You ask your followers to become a part of the giveaway by interacting and engaging with your social media pages. You also ask them to share your social media pages with their friends and families in order to qualify for the giveaway. This way, you serve two important purposes of making your customers happy and also increase the reach of your brand to people who can potentially become your customers in the future.

PRINCIPLES FOR THE E-COMMERCE REVOLUTION:

The revolution of e-commerce was triggered when the Covid-19 pandemic happened. The dramatic increase in sales of the online businesses kick-started an important era of the revolution of e-commerce. Here are a few principles that you have to follow in order to make your business prosper.

1. **CONNECTION WITH CUSTOMERS:**

    You need to connect with your customers in different ways. You can do so by establishing an Omnichannel connection with them, so they are able to shop from your store using both the offline and online shopping methods.

2. BE HONEST:

Always try to remain honest with your customers. Let them know if you are facing some difficulty as a business or if you are running out of stock. Keep them updated with every detail that they should know.

3. PROVIDE YOUR CUSTOMERS WITH CHOICES:

The times are tough so in order to facilitate your customers better you should be flexible with them and provide them with multiple choices while doing any online or offline transactions.

4. KEEP YOURSELF UPDATED:

You should keep on studying your data so you remain updated. You should know what items are in demand by the customers and when you should place orders for the next shipments so your customers do not have to face the issues of products running out of stock. Study your data keenly and try to use it for your own benefits and also for the facilitation of your customers. You can also use polls and collect valuable information regarding your customer support and experience from your customers directly.

All this information will greatly help you in making your business flourish. You need to understand the growing importance of the e-commerce industry. You also need to stay mindful that this trend is not going away any time soon and you should consider it important. You need to come up with ways on how you can make the whole shopping experience of your customers better while also benefitting your business.

CHAPTER 10

Future Of E-Commerce

When many brick-and-mortar businesses have been going through financial challenges and have been struggling to make both their ends meet, the business owners on these online marketplaces have been dealing with great customer traffic. They have been making record sales and generating a lot of profit as a result. This shows that a new era where e-commerce businesses are making a lot of profits has finally started. People have started to understand the importance and the convenience that comes with online shopping. In the pandemic, many companies have been making double sales as compared to their sales from the previous years. The E-commerce industry is flourishing and expanding, thanks to the coronavirus and the havoc it brought upon the whole world. For these online business owners, this coronavirus has been nothing but a blessing in disguise.

From the current situation, it is obvious that the future of e-commerce is very bright. People would still indulge in online shopping even if covid-19 goes away. This is because of the many advantages that come with the idea and practice of online shopping. Online businesses have emerged stronger than ever due to the increased sales that have been happening due to the lockdown and self-quarantine situations. The brands and businesses that work online know how important it is to provide better and improved services to people so they shop from them even when the pandemic is over. They have started working on their customer support programs so they do not lose their clients due to any reason. They have been working tirelessly to introduce new interactive ways of shopping for their customers. Online shopping is very much in demand by people as most of them have been turning towards these online marketplaces. The essential goods, the non-essentials ones, everything is available over these online marketplaces. You just have to see what you need and filter that out from the list of products that are available. The sales have been growing exponentially. Also, it is highly likely that these brick-and-mortar stores close down permanently because the sales that have happened over these online channels have attracted more and more people to start an online business.

Amazon has seen many new people starting their businesses once they have observed the increased number of sales and the profits that have been generated as a result. This whole concept of e-commerce and online shopping is not new to the ears but very much in practice and the impact this has had on the economy of the countries is huge. The economic conditions in most of the countries have been really unstable. It was these online dealings and shopping of people that provided some stability to the economy of most of the countries. As the situation is still uncertain, the behavior of the customers is still volatile and cannot be predicted properly. Thus the business owners are always ready to make adjustments accordingly. They are also keeping up on all the latest trends that people follow so they are prepared for every situation they might face. This is an important reason as to why the future of e-commerce is so bright. In order to make sure that businesses run smoothly with no added pressure, they are working on mitigating the risks that may have come up so they do not waste their time and resources once things go out of hand. They keep on working on these risks and threats accordingly. This will also be a reason that the businesses would be run over by their competitors. As many new business owners have started joining these online marketplaces and have begun launching their products, the competition among different brands has increased multiple folds. This increased competition is playing an important role in maintaining the standards high. Every business is trying to stand out among others by providing world-class products and a shopping experience. This is also a great way in which the whole standard of products is becoming better and improving as a result. This helps with making the the e-commerce industry reach new highs. Also in order to win over their competitors, business owners have started offering sales and discounts on multiple occasions. They have been using this as a marketing strategy to improve their overall business sales but these little steps are also building blocks towards the bright future of the online shopping industry.

Technology also plays a very important role in the development of the e-commerce industry. New and improved websites and apps that use and work on the latest technology have been launched by many businesses also play an important role in the betterment of the future of the online shopping industries. Just as the technology would evolve, new trends and changes would become a part of the e-commerce industry.

Due to all these reasons that have been stated here, it is evident that the future of the online industry is bright and positive. People would still be very much buying and purchasing from these online businesses whether the pandemic stays or not.

Conclusion

The whole concept of the e-commerce industry started when the first devices were built for communication. These devices played an important role in the origination of the e-commerce industry. Slowly and gradually when the technology evolved and the internet was made available to the common public was when the e-commerce industry gathered pace and became an eye candy for people where they can shop while staying inside their houses. The trend was very much followed by people but still, the sales that happened over these online marketplaces were not as flattering as they should have been. A few of the online companies also struggled with their finances because they were not able to achieve the number of sales that they set as their target. Many ups and downs came during this whole journey of online shopping. When the Covid-19 happened and the local governments of different countries announced imposing of lockdowns in order to decrease the spread of the virus. People started to turn more towards these online marketplaces for all the essential and non-essential goods. Many changes came in their lives as the coronavirus came into their lives as well.

They had to adapt to those changes that the coronavirus brought in their lives.

CHANGES THAT CAME WITH THE SPREAD OF CORONAVIRUS:

Online shopping was a new trend that people adapted to as the coronavirus spread rigorously all over the world. Online shopping in these tough and difficult times came with many advantages. Firstly, it allowed people to shop for whatever they wanted from the comfort of their houses, they did not have to leave their houses for anything they needed. Another advantage that online shopping had was that by online shopping they were able to abide by the safety precautions that were issued by the World Health Organization in order to protect people from the threats of coronavirus. People were able to practice the social distancing orders issued to help slow down the spreading of the coronavirus. In short, coronavirus came with many advantages and people started to enjoy this new experience of shopping. This greatly helped them in changing their shopping habits. They no longer went to any brick-and-mortar stores for something that they needed but were able to get everything that they needed, both essential items and non-essential items delivered to their doorstep.

INCREASED TRAFFIC ON THESE ONLINE MARKETPLACES:

The online retailers were not ready for this sudden influx of customer traffic. In the beginning, there were many unfortunate incidents that took place, the customer service of some of the businesses was not up to the mark, many online stores would run out of products because people would buy products in bulk. The online businesses were not prepared for the situation which took place all of a sudden after the brick-and-mortar stores were shut down by the government. Also, there was a delay in deliveries and shipments as the supply chain disruptions were at their peak. Many of the companies that were running in China had to face delays in manufacturing and production because of the coronavirus situation that was getting worse day by day. Not just that but just because some products were in demand and they had gotten scarce, their prices increased as well. There were many issues that these online business owners had to face in the beginning. But since the supply chain disruptions settled and they understood the situation they were in, things started to get better. They also started to make their customer support and service better by coming up with different strategies. They also came up with strategies of retaining their customers and not losing them to any other business. They kept their inventories in check so they don't run out of stock. Many new business owners started to launch their businesses after they saw the increased sales that have happened when the coronavirus on a loose. Many small businesses also launched as a result of the increased sales and profits generated. Great profits were generated by businesses during these times that would last them for some time. Not just that but some of the business owners started to plan the expanding of their businesses over these marketplaces. This gives us the idea that a new era of the e-commerce revolution has begun and it cost us a whole pandemic to understand the importance and need of these online shopping experiences. Now the importance of these marketplaces is understood by people more than ever. They have really gotten used to the whole idea of placing orders without them to leave their houses and get all that they placed orders for delivered at their doorstep. They no longer have to leave their houses and expose themselves to the risks and threats of the coronavirus. Also, many businesses started working on the Omni channel aspects of the businesses. Business owners came up with creative ideas on how they can effectively merge their online business and offline business. This new way of placing orders online and then going to the stores to pick the order instantly without having to wait long was also very much liked and appreciated by the customers.

www.ingramcontent.com/pod-product-compliance
Lightning Source LLC
Chambersburg PA
CBHW060849220526
45466CB00003B/1295